Coming Off Tranquillizers
and Sleeping Pills

Coming Off Tranquillizers and Sleeping Pills

A Withdrawal Plan That Really Works

Shirley Trickett

Thorsons
An Imprint of HarperCollins*Publishers*

Thorsons
An Imprint of HarperCollins*Publishers*
77–85 Fulham Palace Road,
Hammersmith, London W6 8JB.
1160 Battery Street
San Francisco, California 94111-1213.

Published by Thorsons 1986
This completely revised edition published 1991
10 9 8 7 6 5 4 3

A catalogue record for this book
is available from the British Library

ISBN 0 7225 2398 X

Typeset by Harper Phototypesetters Ltd,
Northampton, England
Printed in Great Britain by
HarperCollinsManufacturing Glasgow

Contents

Foreword

This book will become a 'bible' for thousands of men and women who, through no fault of their own, find themselves faced with the problems of benzodiazepine dependence and withdrawal. Many doctors have also turned to it for information and advice on the management of a syndrome still largely uncharted in the medical literature.

Shirley Trickett has done much to draw the attention of the medical profession and the public to the adverse effects of long-term benzodiazepine use and the difficulties of withdrawal. A trained nurse with an understanding of drugs and a talent for applying those skills which help people to help themselves, she has greater experience than most doctors of the range of physical and psychological problems confronting those who wish to come off their tranquillizers. Her efforts led to the instigation of one of Britain's earliest and most effective tranquillizer support groups, 'Come Off It' (1982), which has been the inspiration for similar groups in the UK and abroad. Shirley Trickett's sound clinical judgement and practical advice have already proved invaluable to 500 clients in the North East of England. Doctors too have reason to be grateful to 'Come Off It' for providing their patients with the close personal contact, everyday support, and encouragement that many of them need.

This comprehensive book gives clear descriptions and straightforward explanations of the many symptoms which often bewilder patients undergoing withdrawal, as well as sensible, balanced advice on how to cope with them. Useful tables provide information on drug equivalents and suggested schemes for dosage reduction. Above all, the approach is optimistic with the constant reassurance that the sufferer *will* win through to recovery. Readers throughout the world will be glad of the insight and encouragement they will find in the following pages.

C.H. ASHTON, D.M., F.R.C.P.
Senior Lecturer in Psychopharmacology,
University of Newcastle upon Tyne, England.
Honorary Consultant in Clinical Pharmacology.

Preface
All Withdrawal Symptoms Pass in Time

This book has been written to give comfort and information to those suffering from the problems caused by tranquillizer therapy and withdrawal. It is hoped that it will be a practical guide for those who have not yet started to withdraw, and will also explain some of the strange symptoms experienced by those who have completed withdrawal.

Many of the symptoms are due to increased levels of anxiety due to drug withdrawal, and are not because you are 'silly', 'highly strung', 'neurotic', or 'unable to cope'. If you are well whilst you are taking tranquillizers and have no unpleasant symptoms when you stop taking them, you will not need this information.

Some medical terms have been included to help you understand them if you read them elsewhere.

Withdrawal reactions vary enormously. Some people come off their pills without any problems at all; others have minor discomfort. Those who withdraw abruptly without guidance often have severe problems.

When tranquillizers were first marketed over 30 years ago, doctors were told that they were safe and non-addictive. More recent research has disproved this. In the past few years, valiant efforts have been made by a few top scientists to change medical opinion, but it may take time for the correct information to be accepted by all doctors.

'Release', a London organization which deals mainly with people dependent on hard drugs, has done an enormous amount of work to help tranquillizer victims. They have compiled a national contact list of people who have coped with tranquillizer withdrawal, and are willing to support others. Their pamphlet 'Trouble with Tranquillizers' has given hope to thousands.

It is hoped that as more physicians understand this new abstinence syndrome and are educated in withdrawal management, the situation will dramatically improve. There are after all many alternative ways of dealing with anxiety problems. Some simple ones are discussed in this book.

Shirley Trickett
July 1986

The past four years have seen changes in the use of these drugs but there is still room for improvement. The abundance of information around has caused some doctors to prescribe much more carefully and to support their patients when it is time for withdrawal. Unfortunately, there are *still* doctors who will not open their eyes and see the facts; they continue to claim these drugs are non-addictive and 'mild', they issue repeat prescriptions and pour scorn on suggestions of withdrawal reactions. There are also the 'clean sweep' doctors who, as litigation looms, abruptly withdraw all their patients and refuse to issue any more new prescriptions for these drugs. This causes a great deal of unnecessary suffering both to people withdrawing and also to people who would benefit from short-term, carefully supervised, use of the drugs.

My thoughts on litigation are mixed; whilst I feel that the drug companies, and the doctors who drag people through acute withdrawal or prescribe willy-nilly, should be brought to task, I also feel that where a doctor has 'inherited' large numbers of people on benzodiazepines or where the incident predates current knowledge, it is negative to pursue it. Whilst I also acknowledge the fact that these drugs have damaged countless lives, I also worry about people who will hold themselves back in the quest for retribution; their anger is understandable but it may have to be relinquished before full healing can take place.

In this revised edition I have included my findings on what I see as post-withdrawal problems. Although the effect these drugs have on the immune system is still largely medically overlooked, what I have seen both here and abroad convinces me that this is one of the causes of failure to recover after withdrawal from benzodiazepines. With gratitude I acknowledge the doctors who really listen to their patients and believe what they say no matter how bizarre or untypical their symptoms are. To their blinkered colleagues who need double-blind trials before they tie their shoelaces, and who look down their noses at me if I mention nutritional profiles, chronic Candida or food intolerance, I can only say time will tell – it has in the past: the 'unscientific and anecdotal evidence' of the self-help movement has been found to be remarkably accurate.

Shirley Trickett
Revised edition
March 1990

Introduction

'Am I going mad?' 'Will I ever recover?' These are questions being asked by people experiencing symptoms of tranquillizer withdrawal all over the world. The reply from lay-counsellors who have all been through withdrawal, and from professionals who have knowledge of the problem is: 'No, you are not going crazy,' and 'Yes, you will recover, but it is going to take time.'

These are some of the drugs we will be discussing in this book; when tranquillizers are mentioned it will also mean sleeping pills.

Chemical Name	Brand Name
Diazepam	Valium
Lorazepam	Ativan
Chlordiazepoxide	Librium
Temazepam	Normison, Euhypnos
Oxazepam	Serenid
Triazolam	Halcion
Nitrazepam	Mogadon
Frisium*	Clobazam*

*Not prescribed for anxiety

Part I

1 *There is No Need to Panic*

There is no doubt that tranquillizers help alleviate the distressing symptoms of anxiety. They do not make problems go away, although they can be useful in the short term. Some people tolerate them well and are able to stop them when they feel better. Unfortunately, many users suffer side-effects, and more than 25 per cent experience withdrawal reactions. So, whilst for some the drugs have been a help, for others they have been the start of a distressing experience.

Before you read further in this book, it is very important for you to realize that even if you are severely dependent on the above drugs and have been taking them for 20 years or more, you can still come off them and recover completely from the symptoms caused by withdrawal.

WHO TAKES TRANQUILLIZERS?

The answer is everyone: you, me, the lawyer, the doctor, the taxi driver, the isolated young mum, the frightened young policeman, the menopausal woman, the harassed executive. The list is endless. In the light of more recent information, however, things will change. There will be fewer prescriptions issued, people will be a lot more wary about what they are taking, and will be willing to learn other ways of coping with stress. There are more prescriptions issued to women than men. One reason for this could be that, although it is not the appropriate treatment, many are prescribed for period pain, PMT, baby blues and menopausal problems. Men who take tranquillizers have the same side-effects and withdrawal reactions as women.

SLOW WITHDRAWAL
IS SAFE

By following a careful reduction plan and taking care of your general health, you can come through withdrawal safely. Not only will you feel physically better, but you may be *less* anxious than you were on the drugs. Coming out of the fog of a drugged existence into the world again can be painful at times and you might need time to adjust, but at least you will be really *you*, able to think and feel again.

DRUGS FOR ANXIETY –
BITTER PILLS

Scientists have always been aware of how fear can rule our lives and make us ill and miserable. They have looked for substances to help us to feel calmer and live more normal lives. These chemicals are called *sedatives*. They can certainly help us to feel less fearful and may, *for a time*, enable us to sleep better or function more normally – but at what cost? There is always a catch. We cannot swallow chemicals day after day and expect the body to behave normally. Over the years, it has become apparent that sedatives are of limited use in the long term because of the side-effects and also because of the problems of addiction.

TRANQUILLIZERS AND SLEEPING PILLS (THE BENZODIAZEPINES)

About 30 years ago there was great excitement when scientists thought they had found a substance which did not have the problems of the existing sedatives. This was to become the group of drugs known as the benzodiazepines. They were said to be virtually free from side-effects and to be non-addictive. We now know this is not so – they are highly addictive drugs and the side-effects are numerous. In fact, these drugs are responsible for one of the worst medical blunders of the century. Millions of people worldwide taking no more than normal therapeutic doses are suffering physically and emotionally from the effects of treatment and withdrawal.

How has this happened?

Since the drugs were thought to be non-addictive, when patients reported feeling ill and anxious on stopping them, it was thought that their original anxiety symptoms were coming back. It was not recognized that these symptoms were, in fact, drug withdrawal symptoms. Patients were told to go back to their drugs and, sure enough, the symptoms eased. This is why people continued to take them year after year.

What a puzzle

Many people were very puzzled, saying they were a little anxious before the pills but this could not be compared with the desperate panic they felt when they stopped them.

'But I Was Not Anxious Before I Took Tranquillizers.'
People who have been given tranquillizers as a muscle relaxant for

physical problems, such as back pain, were even more puzzled. Anxiety was not part of their original problem. It is important to understand the physical nature of chemical dependence and also to accept that this has not happened because you lack will-power or guts. In fact, if both were dependent, the 6'3" football player who was prescribed tranquillizers for a knee injury and the middle-aged woman who was prescribed them for her nerves, would experience exactly the same symptoms on withdrawal.

What about people who were anxious before they took the pills? After years on pills they were *still* anxious. So how much was actually caused by the pills and how much by the original anxiety? If they had not taken pills, would they have learned to cope? There have been lots of arguments about this, but one thing is very clear: large numbers of long-term users who have had a history of severe anxiety have been *less* anxious when they have come through withdrawal.

What a long fight

It has taken years of fighting to get where we are today, in that the majority of doctors now realize that normal therapeutic use of these drugs can cause illness and dependence. It is interesting to note that apart from a few stalwart professionals who have been voicing their worries about the drugs for many years, most of the pressure to do something about the problem has come from the public.

ARE THINGS GETTING ANY BETTER?

Happily, yes, but whilst most doctors now follow the suggested guidelines (see Further Information, page 163) there are still some who cannot accept the facts, and either issue prescriptions for ill-advised pharmacological cocktails, or withdraw benzodiazepine prescriptions abruptly and give no support during withdrawal. There has been a spate of this since the media coverage of patients taking legal action over these drugs began.

2 What Are the Side-effects of Sleeping Pills and Tranquillizers?

Drugs are not magic bullets which go only to the target area, but often have unwanted actions elsewhere in the body. These are called side-effects. The side-effects associated with initial use of these pills can include: confusion, dizziness, loss of balance, lack of co-ordination, headaches, skin rashes, speech difficulties, digestive upsets, muscle pains, change of personality, and emotional deadness.

Occasionally, and particularly when the drug is first taken, it can have the opposite effect to the expected one. This is called the paradoxical effect: instead of the muscles being relaxed they can go into spasm, or instead of having a calming effect the drug can act as a stimulant. This can take the form of being 'high' or full of rage.

After a few months' use there is often a confusion of side-effects and withdrawal symptoms. For instance muscle spasm is prominent in withdrawal and it can also appear as a side-effect at the beginning of therapy.

Can I get withdrawal symptoms if I am still taking my pills?

The answer is a very definite 'yes'. Many people have said: 'I have every withdrawal symptom on the list, yet I am still taking my pills.' This is explained later.

CHEMICAL DEPENDENCE

When you take a substance which is not necessary for the normal functioning of the body, such as alcohol, tranquillizers, steroids, caffeine or cigarettes, the body has to adjust to cope with the chemical. If the body relies on the introduced substance to function normally, this is chemical dependence, addiction or habituation.

TOLERANCE

This is when the body gets so used to the substance it needs more and more to keep going. Many people who have taken tranquillizers have become tolerant, and because they did not increase their dosage over the months or years *withdrawal symptoms developed in spite of their taking the full therapeutic dose.* This was the body complaining that the full requirement of the drug was not being taken. Long-term users have often cried with relief when they are given this information. After years and years of mystifying, chronic ill-health, all their strange symptoms are explained at last.

WITHDRAWAL

Withdrawal means reducing or stopping the new substance.

Withdrawal symptoms
If a person becomes physically or nervously ill when deprived of the introduced chemical in sufficient amounts, the problems he experiences are withdrawal symptoms.

3 Withdrawal From Tranquillizers and Sleeping Pills

A NEW WITHDRAWAL SYNDROME*

Whilst some symptoms of tranquilliser withdrawal are common to other withdrawal syndromes, for example nausea and depression, there are many problems such as jaw pain, which seem to be associated only with stopping tranquillizers. This makes the benzodiazepine withdrawal syndrome unique. Perhaps it is because of this that it is taking so long for it to be understood.

Are tranquillizers ever helpful?

Used correctly (see page 163) they are very useful drugs. They can bring great relief from the misery of acute anxiety and give the sufferer a much-needed rest. The danger comes when they are taken for too long – not only because of the side-effects and the risk of dependence, but also because they put the emotions in 'cold storage'. This means the person is unable to react normally to events in their lives, happy or sad – everything is a grey haze. It is rather like putting a plaster on a broken leg; this is useful for a while

*A syndrome is a collection of symptoms.

but if the plaster is kept on, the leg will never get back to normal.

Do all users become dependent?

The answer is 'no', but the reason why some people escape chemical dependence is not understood. It could be that the people who become dependent on tranquillizers are also the people who are allergic to them (or to the dyes or fillers in them). There are many allergic-type symptoms in withdrawal. This would fit with the masked allergy theory of Dr Richard Mackarness, in that daily use of a substance can cause a type of allergy which does not become apparent until your body is denied it. He describes this in his book, *A Little Bit of What You Fancy*, (Fontana, 1985).

● **Even if you feel you aren't dependent, don't stop suddenly.**
Whilst I have said some people do not become dependent, few long-term users, particularly on the short-acting drugs, would be able to stop their drugs acutely and not experience some symptoms.
Please note: *Don't* stop any drug without consulting your doctor and, even if you feel you are not dependent, do not stop suddenly.

Are the withdrawal symptoms sometimes delayed?

Occasionally, yes. Some long-term users who have been on high doses have reported that they stopped abruptly, not knowing it was dangerous, and felt fine for weeks or months before a full-blown withdrawal reaction started. Perhaps this was because they had large amounts of the drug tucked away in their body tissue and this had kept them going.

SIDE-EFFECTS: WHAT DO I RISK IF I STAY ON THE PILLS LONG-TERM?

In view of the more recent information on these drugs, it is unlikely that you would be able to do this, but this is what you risk if you do:

Depression

This is a very common side-effect. If tranquillizers could single out fear and only work on that, things would be fine, but unfortunately, they also damp down the other emotions. This can cause emotional deadness.

Change of personality

Being in an emotionally frozen state can alter the personality. Relatives often complain: 'He hasn't been the same since he took those pills – he's moody, irritable and distant.'

After recovery many users have said, 'It's wonderful to be myself again. At the time I was taking the pills I couldn't see how my personality had changed.'

Chronic vague ill-health

Always being tired, aches and pains, digestive upsets and period problems are common complaints. People who have been on tranquillizers a long time often look drained and miserable. They often wear dark glasses because they cannot bear the light. Newcomers to the tranquillizer groups often look as though they are in uniform: dark glasses and foam rubber neck collars, which they wear to support aching neck muscles.

Thankfully, things don't stay like that and it is wonderful to see people looking healthier and younger as they come through withdrawal – the skin loses its muddy look, the eyes are brighter.

Many have said, 'I'm not sleeping, my neck aches, or I'm burning all the time, but I don't care; I can feel I am coming back to being me.'

Greater risk of accidents

The evidence for this is very clear. There is an increased risk of accidents on the road, operating machinery, and in the home during tranquillizer therapy. The reason must be lack of concentration and co-ordination.

Increased risk of violence

These drugs are known to cause lack of inhibition, aggression and outbursts of rage. This can lead to violent behaviour which includes baby-battering, assault, homicide and suicide.

Many people on these drugs have been accused of shoplifting. This is not surprising, since they cause such confusion. There have also been people charged with being drunk and disorderly when they haven't taken alcohol. Over-sedation and confusion can occur when the effect of night sedation lingers and a 'daytime' tranquillizer such as Valium is taken.

Tranquillizers and babies

Taking tranquillizers in the first six weeks of pregnancy has been linked to an increase in the incidence of cleft lip and cleft palate. Another study (Hartz, S.C., et al. 'Antenatal exposure to meprobamate and chlordiazepoxide in relation to malformations, mental development, and childhood mortality'. *New Eng. J. Med.* 1982; 292:726–728) refutes this, but the evidence has caused enough concern for the FDA (US Food and Drug Administration) to say that using Valium in pregnancy 'should almost always be avoided'.

Floppy baby syndrome
Using these drugs late in pregnancy may result in babies being weak and having feeding or breathing difficulties.

Withdrawal symptoms in the newborn
This has been widely reported in mothers who took tranquillizers continuously in late pregnancy. The babies have muscle spasm, are restless and are generally more difficult to manage than infants in heroin withdrawal.

Tranquillizers and the elderly

Because the elderly excrete these drugs less efficiently, there is often a buildup which leads to toxic confusion. This can be mistaken for senility. Carefully lowering the dose often dramatically improves this. There is also the danger of loss of balance leading to hip fractures. It is often better not to take elderly long-term users through complete withdrawal; lowering the dose can be enough to improve symptoms.

INTERACTION WITH OTHER DRUGS

Because they are both 'downers', alcohol and tranquillizers are a bad combination. They can lead to over-sedation, depression and accidental death. This can also happen with: antidepressants, antihistamines, major tranquillizers, barbiturates, epilepsy drugs, and narcotics.

Have I damaged myself permanently through taking tranquillizers?

Hundreds of tearful people ask this question. The good news is that the human body has a wonderful capacity for putting things right even if it has been very badly treated. Once the poisons leave your body, things will slowly get back to normal. You have everything inside yourself necessary for self-healing and how quickly you recover is going to depend on you – you are in the driving seat. That is not to say you won't need guidance and support: you will, but you're the only one who can do the work necessary to recover. This will be explained later.

4 How Do I Know If I Am Dependent?

If you feel ill, sick, shaky, 'high', anxious or depressed when you try to cut down your pills, and if the feelings go away when you take them again, then you could be dependent.

How do I know I am not just imagining the symptoms?

If you have felt that the pills have supported you through bad times, then there may be some anxiety at the thought of stopping them; however, it is unlikely that worries over stopping would cause such dramatic symptoms and, as mentioned earlier, some of the withdrawal symptoms have nothing to do with anxiety.

Hospital Research Supports This

We know from clinical tests that it is not a matter of 'Oh dear, I haven't had my Valium today – I am going to feel awful'. It is the body complaining when it does not get the chemical it needs. In the tests, people were given dummy tablets which looked exactly the same as the ones they had been taking, so they were unaware they were withdrawing and yet they developed withdrawal symptoms. We also know this from the people who are withdrawn in outpatient pharmacology (prescribed drugs) clinics. They are given their drug in suspension: a bottle of pink medicine. One spoonful might contain 2mg or 10mg – they don't know when they are being reduced, and yet their symptoms always peak at the expected time.

WHAT HAPPENS IF I AM DEPENDENT?

You must see your doctor and say you would like to withdraw slowly from your pills. He may be well-informed about withdrawal and support you all the way. Although this might sound like a fairy tale to some people, it does happen. There *are* some physicians who are concerned about this problem.

Others are honest, and admit they know nothing about withdrawal, but are willing to do their best. They look for information and encourage their patients to find a self-help group.

However there are the well-meaning, but ill-informed ones who say: 'But Mrs Frail, you have always been an anxious person, you need these pills.' If this is said to you, your reply could be: 'But doctor, the pills are not working now, they are making me more anxious (see page 150). I want to learn other ways of coping with my nerves.'

Unhappily, some people have met with hostility: 'So *you're* the doctor now – you know better than I do. Come off your pills then – no more prescriptions for you.'

Some have not even got as far as the doctor. When they have telephoned for a repeat prescription the receptionist has curtly told them: 'Dr Hastie has stopped all prescriptions for tranquillizers and sleeping pills.'

Information for doctors

The latest guidelines for professionals are included (page 163) for those who have trouble convincing their medical practitioners that these drugs can cause problems.

WHAT DO I DO IF IT IS AN EMERGENCY?

If you are on a small dose – say up to 5mg diazepam daily – and are not a featherweight or severely undernourished, it might be uncomfortable but not dangerous to stop abruptly, you may have no choice but to wait until after office hours and call an emergency doctor. He will often give you enough to keep you going until you can change your doctor. Some people have gone to hospital emergency departments.

When should I start withdrawing?

Don't rush into it before an event likely to be stressful: getting married, moving house, changing your job etc. Wait until life is quieter and, if possible, prepare for it by changing to a less hectic routine, learning about relaxation, eating well and generally looking after your health. More about this later.

How should I cut down?

You are the only one who knows what it feels like to be inside your body, so the rate at which you withdraw should, ideally, be your choice. Some people prefer slow withdrawal, others get impatient and like to speed it up. In general, slow withdrawal is more popular and many people carry on perfectly normally as they cut down; they do stressful jobs, look after families and so on. More rapid withdrawal is chosen when the side-effects (poisonous effects) are too severe to cope with, when the person has a lot of support and can take it easy, or when the user is impatient to be drug-free.

The tables given in chapter 5 are only a guide; adjust them to your needs. Reductions can be made every two or four weeks. You might think you can cut corners – 'I am feeling fine, I can go faster than this,' or 'work is busy over the next few months; I think I will slow down.' What you must *not* do is to make the blood levels of the drug unstable – up one minute and down the next. You will increase your symptoms if you do this; you push yourself in and out of withdrawal.

Some people say: 'I knew the meeting on Wednesday was going to be stressful, so I saved my morning pill and took it with the lunchtime one, or I wanted a good sleep before the journey so I missed two nights before and took a full dose on Tuesday.' Your body does not like this and it may take several days to adjust.

5 Slow Withdrawal Tables

DIAZEPAM
15mg daily (7½×2mg tablets)

Week	Morning	Lunchtime	Evening	No. of tablets daily
1	2 tablets	1½ tablets	2 tablets	= 5½
3	1¼ tablets	1¼ tablets	1½ tablets	= 4
5	1 tablet	1 tablet	1 tablet	= 3
7	¾ tablet	¾ tablet	¾ tablet	= 2½
9	½ tablet	½ tablet	¾ tablet	= 1¾
11	½ tablet	¼ tablet	½ tablet	= 1¼
13	¼ tablet	¼ tablet	¼ tablet	= ¾
15	⅛ tablet	⅛ tablet	¼ tablet	= ½
17	⅛ tablet	—	⅛ tablet	= ¼
19	⅛ tablet	—	—	= ⅛

Some people reduce every two weeks at the beginning and then every four weeks as they near the end of withdrawal. If you are on more than 15mg of diazepam you might want to speed things up. You could drop 5mg every two weeks until you are down to 15mg then follow the above table.

Withdrawal from diazepam can be smoother than from some of the other drugs because it stays longer in the body. For this reason, and also because they are easier to cut up, some people are changed from the drugs they are taking, e.g. Ativan to an *equivalent* dose of diazepam.

This is done over a period of one to two weeks. For example, the lunchtime dose could be changed to diazepam for a few days, then the morning dose and so on. It is important to get the correct equivalent dose and accept that there may be a little withdrawal changeover reaction. Many people have been much happier with this method. People on more than 6mg of lorazepam might not need the full equivalent dose of diazepam.

Here are the figures for diazepam substitution from the *Drug Newsletters, Northern Regional Health Authority (Newcastle upon Tyne), No. 31, April, 1985.*

Dose (mg) equivalent to 10mg diazepam

Chlordiazepoxide 25mg	=	diazepam	10mg
Lorazepam 1–2mg	=	diazepam	10mg
Nitrazepam 10mg	=	diazepam	10mg
Oxazepam 20mg	=	diazepam	10mg
Temazepam 20mg	=	diazepam	10mg

NB. *These dose equivalents are only approximate and adjustment to patients' individual requirements may be needed.*

LORAZEPAM
3×1mg tablets

Week	Morning	Lunchtime	Evening	No. of tablets daily
1	1 tablet	½ tablet	1 tablet	= 2½
3	1 tablet	½ tablet	½ tablet	= 2
5	½ tablet	½ tablet	½ tablet	= 1½
7	½ tablet	¼ tablet	½ tablet	= 1¼

Week	Morning	Lunchtime	Evening	No.
9	½ tablet	¼ tablet	¼ tablet	= 1
11	¼ tablet	¼ tablet	¼ tablet	= ¾
13	⅛ tablet	⅛ tablet	⅛ tablet	= ⅜
15	⅛ tablet	—	⅛ tablet	= ¼
17	⅛ tablet	—	—	= ⅛

½mg tablets of lorazepam should be available in the near future.

OXAZEPAM
60mg daily (10mg tablets)

Week	Morning	Lunchtime	Evening	No. of tablets daily
1	2 tablets	1 tablet	2 tablets	= 5
3	1½ tablets	1 tablet	2 tablets	= 4½
5	1½ tablets	1 tablet	1½ tablets	= 4
7	1 tablet	1 tablet	1½ tablets	= 3½
9	1 tablet	1 tablet	1 tablet	= 3
11	1 tablet	½ tablet	1 tablet	= 2½
13	½ tablet	½ tablet	1 tablet	= 2
15	½ tablet	½ tablet	½ tablet	= 1½
17	¼ tablet	¼ tablet	½ tablet	= 1
19	¼ tablet	¼ tablet	¼ tablet	= ¾
21	¼ tablet	—	¼ tablet	= ½
22	¼ tablet	—	—	= ¼

CHLORDIAZEPOXIDE
30mg daily (5mg capsules)

Week	Morning	Lunchtime	Evening	No. of capsules daily
1	2 capsules	1 capsule	2 capsules	= 5
3	1½ capsules	1 capsule	1½ capsules	= 4

5	1 capsule	1 capsule	1½ capsules	= 3½
7	1 capsule	1 capsule	1 capsule	= 3
9	1 capsule	½ capsule	1 capsule	= 2½
11	½ capsule	½ capsule	1 capsule	= 2
13	½ capsule	½ capsule	½ capsule	= 1½
15	½ capsule	—	½ capsule	= 1
17	½ capsule	—	—	= ½

Some powders irritate the throat. To avoid this, open the capsule, divide the powder, and then fit it together again. Some pharmacists are willing to do this for you. If this is not possible you can buy empty capsules and fill them with divided doses of the powder.

TRIAZOLAM
250 Micrograms nightly (two 125 microgram tablets)

This is a very short-acting drug and for this reason it causes a lot of problems. Some people have suffered severe depression, suicidal feelings and jaw pain after taking this drug for only two weeks. These symptoms resolve quite quickly when the drug is withdrawn. If you have these problems you might wish to change over to diazepam for withdrawal, or if you prefer you could follow the plan below:

Week	Nightly dose
1	2 tablets
3	1½ tablets
5	1 tablet
7	½ tablet
9	¼ tablet

TEMAZEPAM
20mg nightly (10mg capsules*)

This is quite an awkward one to cut down. If you don't want to change over to diazepam, you can prick the capsule with a darning needle and squeeze out all the jelly inside. From this you can see how much there is, and estimate how much of the jelly you want to discard. It could be approximately half or quarter or whatever you choose. You could make these reductions every two or four weeks:

Week	Daily
1	1½
3	1¼
5	1
7	¾
9	½
11	¼

If you wanted to withdraw more rapidly, Temazepam is now available in a planned reduction pack** – a two weeks' supply of 10mg capsules, a two weeks' supply of 5mg capsules, and a two weeks' supply of 2mg capsules. Unfortunately, these smaller doses are not available except in the packs.

NITRAZEPAM
10mg nightly
(two×5mg tablets)

Week	Nightly dose
1	1½ tablets

*Now also in 10mg and 20mg tablets

**CAUTION The withdrawal regime in the planned reduction pack can be too rapid for the long-term user.

3	1 tablet
5	¾ tablet
7	½ tablet
9	¼ tablet
11	⅛ tablet

If preferred, these reductions could be made every four weeks.

EXAMPLE OF RAPID WITHDRAWAL

Diazepam 15mg (7½ × 2mg tablets)

Week	Morning	Lunchtime	Evening	Daily
1	2 tablets	2 tablets	2 tablets	= 6
2	1½ tablets	1½ tablets	1½ tablets	= 4½
3	1 tablet	1 tablet	1 tablet	= 3
4	½ tablet	½ tablet	½ tablet	= 1½

For a dose of 30mg of diazepam, six weeks is the minimum withdrawal period recommended.

Remember: do not compare the number of milligrams (mg). 1mg of one drug cannot be substituted for 1mg of another drug. 5mg of chlordiazepoxide (Librium) does not equal 5mg of diazepam, etc.

- If the drug you are on is not mentioned in these tables just apply to same principles for cutting down. The suggested reductions have been calculated to make it as convenient as possible to divide the doses. Another way to do it is to cut down by approximately one eighth of the daily dose every two to four weeks; for example, if you were on a dose of 40mg you could reduce by 5mg and then two to four weeks later you could reduce by 4mg.

6 Withdrawal Symptoms

If you consider what the drugs do (control anxiety, relax nerves and muscles, help you sleep, and slow down heartbeats and breathing) it is understandable that your body will complain loudly when they are cut down or stopped. Don't be alarmed by the following list of symptoms. You may only experience a couple of them, particularly if you reduce carefully and take care of yourself. Even if you feel that what you are experiencing is withdrawal, all persistent symptoms, for example abdominal or chest pain, should be checked by your physician.

- Increased anxiety
- Panic attacks
- Fears of going mad
- Insomnia; nightmares
- Increased depression
- Suicidal feelings
- Agoraphobia
- Aggression
- Outbursts of rage
- Symptoms like 'flu
- Tight throat
- Nausea
- Abdominal pain
- Constipation; Diarrhoea
- Hyperactivity
- Craving for tablets
- Hallucinations (seeing or hearing things)
- Distorted vision
- Confusion
- Dizziness
- Sweating
- Shaking
- Palpitations, slow pulse
- Tight chest
- Chest pain

- Tingling around mouth, hands, and feet
- Breathless feeling
- Increased sensitivity to light, sound, touch, and smell
- Loss of taste; metallic taste
- Ringing in the ears
- Feelings of tight band around head
- Feelings of electricity all over
- Headaches
- Sinus problems
- Pain in the neck and shoulders
- Heavy aching limbs
- Pins and needles
- Jelly legs

- Sore eyes
- Blurred vision
- Creeping sensation in the skin
- Skin rashes
- Loss of interest in sex; impotence
- Dramatic increase in sexual feelings
- Hormone problems
- Thyroid problems
- Pain in the face or jaw which resembles toothache
- Fits have been reported, but **only** when drugs have been stopped abruptly

All withdrawal symptoms pass in time

Accepting some withdrawal symptoms as part of getting better could shorten your recovery time. Try to see a new symptom as a positive step nearer to a drug-free life. After all, the symptoms mean your body is getting rid of poison. What about the mental poison too? If you fret and fume and become obsessed by thoughts of suing your doctor or the drug company, you are only going to hold yourself back. Nothing is more important than your health. Doctors are not immune from the problem themselves; they become dependent too. Several have contacted self-help groups for support for themselves. Don't forget, doctors have anxiety problems too. A report some years ago suggested that if the doctor suffered from anxiety, he was more likely to prescribe tranquillizers for his patients.

Take it slowly

You must also accept that it is going to take time. It might have taken you years to get into this state. It will not go overnight, although you will see improvements even in the early days.

HOW LONG WILL THE WITHDRAWAL SYMPTOMS LAST?

Everyone wants to know this, but there is no easy answer because it varies so much. It will depend on the drug you have been on, how long you have taken it, and, very importantly, how long it takes your body to get back to normal. Don't forget, this includes your nerves – they are not separate, existing somewhere outside you; they are in there with bones, muscles and other tissue. Nervous tissue takes longer than bone and muscle to heal. People are often unaware of this and expect to be completely well as soon as they are drug-free. Nature does not heal in a straight line – there are ups and downs, so don't be discouraged if you feel really well then have another dip; this is very much to be expected.

Many people have been told that the withdrawal symptoms only last a few weeks. Not only is this not true, it is also very worrying for the sufferer. They know they do not feel right and become convinced there is something else wrong with them.

Some people feel much better in a few weeks, for others it can be months, whilst still others may not be fully recovered for two or three years. A great deal is going to depend on how much care you take of yourself. It will also depend on how much emotional pain has been suppressed by the pills. As the drugs leave your body, old pain often surfaces and needs to be dealt with. Again, this is to be welcomed. The mind also wants to heal itself; it only needs a little co-operation from you. Don't be upset if you feel tearful or angry about things which happened years ago; just let them surface when they need to. In time, if you can really let the past go and forgive those who have hurt you, this will bring great healing.

Learning about withdrawal

Some professionals feel information about withdrawal should not be given to patients. They say: 'Show people a list of symptoms and they will imagine they have them.' My experience is the opposite: if people have full information about the symptoms, can be regularly reassured, and accept that they will pass, they relax and do very much better.

'I'll get by with a little help from my friends'

Explain to your family and friends what you are doing and show them any information you have. They will be more supportive if they know what is happening. Partners often gain as much from tranquillizer self-help groups as the sufferers themselves. They learn that we are all hurt inside, and find that coming together to share feelings can be a great relief.

Withdrawal neurosis

A minority of people have developed what could be termed withdrawal neurosis – they are totally bound up in withdrawal and refuse to reach out to normality. Some people cling to the withdrawal label to justify how they feel. They are often people who have very unhappy lives, or people who have an investment in staying ill. It might keep a daughter at home, stop a wife from leaving her husband, or protect the sufferers from looking at what is really going on in their emotional lives.

Where do all the withdrawal symptoms come from?

Tranquillizers make you less anxious, you sleep better, your heart rate and breathing are slower, your movements and thinking are slower, your emotions are pushed down, you feel less, your senses are dulled, your muscles are relaxed, and your blood sugar levels are higher. This means *your adrenaline levels are low.*

When you come off them too quickly your anxiety soars, you can't sleep, your heart rate and breathing speed up, you become hyperactive, your thoughts go wild, your trapped emotions come pouring out, your senses become frighteningly normal, your muscles tighten and hurt, and your blood sugar falls. This means *your adrenaline levels are sky-high.* Is it surprising people think they are going mad?

7 Anxiety

Clinical tests have proved that anxiety (and therefore adrenaline) levels after the drugs have been stopped can rise to levels six times greater than pre-withdrawal levels. Remember that this happens even if people do not know they are being withdrawn.

Tranquillizers seem to stop the part of the brain that deals with anxiety from working – but what really happens is that the anxiety simmers away under the 'lid' of the drugs and when the lid is taken off, all the emotions boil over. This emotional explosion is temporary and *you will return to normal*.

The first step in dealing with the anxiety symptoms is to truly accept that this is what is causing your problems. Many people say: 'But this could not possibly be just anxiety – I feel as if I am dying.' This is just how acute anxiety can make you feel, but there is a great deal you can do to help yourself; you can work with your body to stop so much adrenaline being produced.

To illustrate how many (although it is agreed not all) of the withdrawal symptoms are due to high anxiety/adrenaline levels, here is a quote from 'Anxiety Neurosis' from the *Oxford Textbook of Psychiatry* (1983), Ed. Gelder, Gath and Mayou. Don't take any notice of the word 'neurosis'. Although it is often used as a 'put down' it should not be; it simply means behaviour caused by trapped hurts and we all have those – we are all neurotic.

Anxiety neuroses have psychological and physical symptoms. The psychological symptoms are the familiar feeling of fearful anticipation that gives the condition its name, irritability, difficulty in concentration, sensitivity to noise, and a feeling of restlessness. Patients often complain of poor memory when they are really experiencing the effects of failure to concentrate.

Repetitive thoughts form an important part of an anxiety neurosis. These are often provoked by awareness of autonomic over-activity; e.g. a patient who feels his heart beating fast may worry about having a heart attack. Thoughts of this kind probably prolong the condition.

The appearance of a person with an anxiety neurosis is characteristic. His or her face looks strained, with a furrowed brow; the posture is tense; he or she is restless and often tremulous. The skin looks pale, and sweating is common especially from the hands, feet and axillae [armpits – explanations of medical words do not appear in original article].

Readiness to tears, which may at first suggest depression, reflects a generally apprehensive state. The physical symptoms and signs of an anxiety neurosis result from either over-activity in the sympathetic nervous system or in increased tension in the skeletal muscles.

The list of symptoms is long, and is conveniently grouped by systems of the body. Symptoms related to the gastro-intestinal tract include dry mouth, difficulty in swallowing, epigastric discomfort [under breastbone], excessive wind caused by aerophagy [air swallowing], borborygmi [rumbling of intestinal gases], and frequent loose motions.

Common respiratory symptoms include a feeling of constriction in the chest, difficulty in inhaling (which contrasts with the expiratory difficulty in asthma), and over-breathing and its consequences [which are described later].

Cardiovascular symptoms include palpitations, a feeling of discomfort or pain over the heart, awareness of missed beats, and throbbing in the neck.

Common genito-urinary symptoms are increased frequency and urgency of micturition]act of passing urine], failure of erection, and lack of libido. Women may complain of increased menstrual discomfort and sometimes amenorrhoea]absence of periods].

Complaints related to the functions of the central nervous system include tinnitus, blurring of vision, prickling sensations, and dizziness (which is not rotational).

Other symptoms may be related to muscular tension. In the scalp, this may be experienced as aching or stiffness, especially in the back and shoulders. The hands may tremble so that delicate movements are impaired.

In anxiety neuroses sleep is disturbed in a characteristic way. On going to bed, the patient lies awake worrying; when at last he falls asleep, he wakes intermittently. He often reports un-pleasant dreams.

As you can see, we are dealing with something that does not only happen in withdrawal. These feelings can be experienced by people who have never had drugs.

It is a pity more professionals don't have the time to explain the awful physical feelings and mental turmoil caused by being over-anxious. Taking the mystery away knocks it down to size.

What happens in the body when you are over-anxious?

Flooded with adrenaline

Whatever the cause – it could be worries at work, chronic physical pain, withdrawal or nervous exhaustion – your adrenaline levels will be too high. We need adrenaline in normal amounts to function, and at times in large amounts to give us a spurt of energy to run from danger etc. What we don't need is to be flooded with too much of it all the time; it makes us feel ill and frightened.

Which symptoms will go when adrenaline levels go down?

A great many, not only the physical ones: sweating, shaking, churning stomach, palpitations, running to the loo, etc, but also panic attacks, feelings of gloom and doom, suicidal feelings, obsessions, feelings of unreality, confusion, lack of concentration, paranoia, irritability.

Before anxiety symptoms are discussed, some common worries will be explained.

What does it feel like to have too much adrenaline?

Because the whole body is stimulated, everything is speeded up. This can result in an increase in movement and accelerated thoughts and speech. Bodily functions are speeded up too – heart rate, breathing and digestion – hence the running to the loo.

Feelings of gloom and doom

All the feelings caused by being over-anxious are unpleasant, but the hardest to cope with are the wayward thoughts which become distorted and gloomy. More about this later.

8 Have My Senses Taken Leave of Me?

We all have a part of the brain that normally works to allow us to be anxious when necessary. During stress (which would certainly include withdrawal) this mechanism may become over-stimulated, so we become over-anxious.

The body reacts to the chemicals poured into the bloodstream, and this gives us the distressing physical feelings which we associate with anxiety: heart beating wildly, stomach churning, shaking and sweating etc.

If your arm was injured and needed rest, you would put it in a sling. You can learn to give your exhausted nervous system the same kind of comfort and rest by accepting that you are nervously ill, looking after your body and letting time pass. This may sound difficult, particularly if you are coping with misery in your life. However, the advice is sound. If you fight your symptoms, you will further stimulate your over-sensitized nerves, and end up even more exhausted and ill. Accepting your fear may be the hardest thing you have ever done, but think of the rewards.

If you have a weak chest, catching a chill or getting over-tired could result in bronchitis. In the same way, if your nerves are over-strained, an unexpected gas bill or even a door banging may make you feel ill.

DEPERSONALIZATION

This can happen when anxiety levels are high. People who have never had medication can also suffer this. Perhaps this is the main symptom that makes people think they are going crazy. This is understandable because they feel they are not real, not in touch with themselves, and they worry that their mental processes are going to break down completely. Many say: 'I look in the mirror and I know it's me, but it doesn't look like me – I don't recognize myself.' It could be that the anxiety feelings are too much to cope with so you retreat into 'not being you'. If this is very severe the sufferers may hallucinate, 'seeing' themselves or their face. All these feelings or images disappear as the anxiety levels come down.

DE-REALIZATION

This means not feeling in touch with reality, and feeling strange in familiar surroundings. People say: 'I walk into my kitchen and it looks totally different.' Again, these feelings mean your anxiety levels are high. Keep remembering these feelings are coming because of chemical reactions in your body – withdrawal from the tranquillizers is raising your adrenaline levels. The feelings will go in time, but if you are having them regularly you may have to cut down more slowly or take more rest.

HALLUCINATIONS

If you are cutting down slowly, these should not trouble you. People are much less afraid when they understand that this is happening because they are withdrawing too quickly. The looming faces so often seen, are really just an exaggeration of what normally happens as we are dropping off to sleep, although we are rarely aware of it. Just as in alcohol withdrawal, people 'see' spiders, reptiles, devils etc. One woman 'saw' her father so clearly she made him a cup of coffee. He was three hundred miles away at the time.

She slowed down her withdrawal and had no further hallucinations. Hearing music, voices or telephones ringing is often
reported. These too disappear when withdrawal is slowed down.

PERCEPTION DIFFICULTIES

Some of the action of the drug is on the temporal lobe area of the
brain; during withdrawal this area is trying to get back to normal,
and for a time this may result in temporal lobe symptoms, including
perception difficulties. This means your senses (sight, sound,
touch, taste and smell) may appear to be playing tricks on you. Your
senses have been dulled by the drugs for so long that you have
gradually become accustomed to altered perception – rather like
being in a grey room where the amount of light and sound does
not change. It is understandable that after withdrawal space seems
vast, colours alarmingly bright and traffic seems deafening and
speeded up. You will slowly adjust to this and realize this was how
the world looked before you took tranquillizers. Light and colours
can seem so bright that some people have to wear dark glasses for
a while. (Please note it is not a good idea to continuously deprive
the eyes of light; see page 143.) Many people have forgotten the
pleasure of colour and are thrilled by their gardens. Before withdrawal one woman kept scrubbing her carpet, thinking it was dull.
When she came off her drugs she said she felt the colours were
leaping out at her, they were so bright. If you see a mark on the wall
as a beetle or a coat hanging up as a person, these are perception
difficulties. If you see these things when there is no mark on the wall
or coat on the door, then these could be hallucinations. Many
people say faces seem to change when they look at them or
buildings seem to be at an angle or to appear too tall and thin.
These are temporary disturbances and will go in time. Check your
breathing (page 120): over-breathing heightens perception.

Sound

The hypersensitivity to sound causes a lot of family arguments. The sufferer has to turn the sound on the television so low that no one else can hear it. Doorbells are often disconnected, and telephones covered with blankets or cushions to deaden the noise. Even sounds not normally noticed like the click of a light switch, or a clock ticking, can seem distressingly loud to the sufferer.

Touch

Even the lightest touch causes some people pain. Others do not feel pain, but say everything feels strange – water feels like slime or jelly, objects that should feel rough feel smooth, and often the finger tips are so sensitive that it causes discomfort to touch a rough fabric.

Taste

Some people lose their sense of taste altogether. Others complain of altered taste sensation. It may be a surprise to find chocolate tasting salty or something like meat tasting sweet, but it is only a temporary nuisance. A metallic taste, sweet or bitter taste in the mouth is a common complaint.

Smell

Some users report loss of smell, but others say even pleasant smells like perfume become so overpowering they are unpleasant. One man said he had a smell like petrol in his nose for weeks.

EYE PROBLEMS

Sore eyes, blurred or double vision and increased sensitivity to light are common, but because the use of these drugs has been associated with an increase in the pressure of the fluid within the eye, you should see your oculist to have it checked out. When you have confirmed that you do not need treatment, just relax; your vision will improve as withdrawal progresses. Users often change their spectacles several times during withdrawal without much effect.

✓ PANIC ATTACKS

The majority of the distress calls to tranquillizer help lines are about panic attacks.

These are characterized by sudden intense feelings of anxiety often associated with feelings of impending death or disaster and fear of going mad. Unpleasant physical feelings are also present. These include palpitations, dizziness, nausea, shaking, choking sensations, feelings of unreality, an urgent need for the bathroom, hot and cold flushes and pins and needles. The attacks can last seconds or minutes or, more rarely, hours. They are unpleasant but not dangerous. More about panic attacks and how to cope with them on page 123.

OBSESSIONS

Obsessions are persistent thoughts or images which the sufferer feels powerless to get rid of, even if they know they are silly or unpleasant. This is a common withdrawal problem; anxiety does funny things to us. Mild obsessions are common even in healthy people – a line of a song or part of an old conversation going around and around in the head. In withdrawal people sometimes have unpleasant thoughts about their nearest and dearest. Although they feel upset and guilty about such thoughts they can't get rid of them.

Compulsions

When the anxiety caused by obsessive thoughts becomes severe, the sufferer changes his behaviour in an attempt to cope. This is called *compulsive behaviour*: actions, or avoidance of actions, that don't make sense to the sufferer or onlookers. For example a person may be convinced he has not turned the gas off or locked the door and might have to check a dozen times before he can be sure he has done it. People laugh about this when they are better.

SUICIDAL FEELINGS

In withdrawal, suicidal feelings can come 'out of the blue'. Some people don't get them at all, while others get vague feelings, and some feel they are at risk. If you are worried see your physician as soon as possible. He may want you to take an antidepressant drug for a time or he may be able to direct you to a counselling service.

Many callers say, 'I have a wonderful family. Why do I have such feelings?' Over-strained nerves often provoke suicidal feelings, but in withdrawal it could also indicate you are cutting down too quickly.

The Samaritans are always there to help. Many people say, 'I had awful suicidal feelings but I didn't feel I could telephone because I knew they were only feelings and I would not do anything.' People give up their time to comfort and support sufferers, so don't hesitate to use them if you need to talk. Directory enquiries will give you the number if you cannot find it in the telephone book.

OUTBURSTS OF RAGE

This can happen as a side-effect and a withdrawal reaction. Mothers are often afraid they will hurt their children during these moments. Losing your temper out of all proportion to the situation is distressing and very common. Give those around you all the literature you have on withdrawal to help them to understand that what you are experiencing is temporary and not your real personality.

SHAKING

Visible shaking, or a feeling of shaking inside, is common. This is to be expected when adrenaline levels are high and, like all the other symptoms, will disappear when your nervous system recovers. The shaking inside may be due to low blood sugar, too much caffeine or too many cigarettes. What to do about this is on page 127.

LACK OF CONCENTRATION

People in withdrawal say: 'How is it that I'm having difficulty doing simple things I have done all my life?' One said 'It has taken me two hours to replace a washer on the tap'. Poor memory is another problem, although there is some confusion between memory lapses and loss of concentration. Many people have said that they make appointments and then forget them. It may be that because they are so tense, they fail to take the information in at the time, rather than that they have subsequently forgotten it. Concentration does improve as withdrawal progresses. Life can be very boring when you cannot concentrate to read or watch television. Some people find large print books from the library helpful.

HYPERACTIVITY

The aimless hyperactivity experienced by some can be very hard to live with (and to watch). The constant desire to move is exhausting but, unfortunately, the energy cannot be utilized; the sufferer usually wanders about doing a small part of one task, then another, without achieving anything. One caller said 'I wash two plates, then find myself putting laundry away. Two minutes later I am sweeping the path. I feel all speeded up but my mind won't let me use the energy productively.'

Pressure of thought and speech

This is part of being hyperactive. Endless conversations (sometimes from years before) or the same line of a TV commercial or song can go around and around in your head. Relatives often complain that the user has become completely self-centred, talking incessantly about the drugs and withdrawal symptoms. But people *do* regain their own personality when they are well.

INSOMNIA

The rebound insomnia experienced in withdrawal can be severe. Your normal sleeping pattern may not return for weeks or months. Try to accept this; it will return to normal eventually.

Even people who are well and not on drugs, night workers for instance, can have disturbing symptoms, such as depersonalization (not being in touch with themselves), and de-realization (not being in touch with reality) when they are deprived of sleep.

Preparation for a good night's sleep starts when you get up. If you are hyperactive because you are in drug withdrawal it is unrealistic to expect the adrenaline levels to drop just because it is your bedtime. You must work with your body during the day to bring the levels of this hormone down. The instructions are on page 139.

Dreams and nightmares

The dreams and nightmares you may be flooded with during withdrawal are just a sign that the 'computer' in your brain is working hard to get things back to normal. It is sorting out a backlog of jumbled emotions which have been suppressed whilst you have been on drugs. People are often alarmed by the nature of the dreams. They include violence, disaster and disturbed sexual behaviour. Be assured they *will* pass as withdrawal progresses. Recounting the dreams or writing them down when you wake sometimes helps to make you less anxious about them. Although it might seem childish, when you wake, get into the habit of giving your dream a satisfactory ending; for instance, if you are being chased by a bull, imagine you have total control, and that when you clap your hands a silver horse appears and carries you to safety. Or if you are walking naked down a busy street, imagine a stranger covers your confusion and shame with a beautiful silver cloak, making the stares of the onlookers turn to respectful glances. Be in charge. If you deal with your dreams this way it often stops you carrying around feelings of fear or low self-esteem all day.

Those who suffer withdrawal insomnia say it is the most difficult symptom to cope with. So often it is said: 'If only I could get a good night's sleep, I could cope with the days.' Sleeping only a couple of hours a night in early withdrawal is not uncommon. Although it is very hard to bear, try not to become too anxious about it. Withdrawal insomnia is a particularly severe form of insomnia. Allowing time and taking care of your nerves will lead to recovery.

Other causes of insomnia in withdrawal

There are factors other than high adrenaline levels which cause sleeping problems. These include muscle and joint problems, itching and burning skin and bowel problems (particularly a disturbance of the balance of the bacteria in the bowel). These will be discussed later in the book.

A deep relaxation session is worth four hours' sleep and it is useful to practise morning and early evening, (page 139) but if you can't or won't make time, build relaxation sessions into your day and if you are having difficulty 'dropping off', get up and do some slow stretching exercises, massage the soles of your feet really firmly or lie in a warm bath to rest your muscles. Some people have herb tea or a milk drink. Go back to bed and breathe slowly and gently, raising the abdomen as you inhale (page 121); continue for half an hour. Some people find it helpful to listen to a relaxation tape, particularly with a headset. This cuts out external noise and also stops you disturbing your partner, but do remember that this cannot replace your daytime slowing-down programme.

9 *Depression*

You may feel delighted that you have managed to cut down or stop taking your pills, yet feel puzzled by how 'down' you feel. Most drug withdrawal is associated with depression. You have to remember that your brain chemistry has been disturbed: this is another temporary state to endure. It will improve or disappear altogether when you are through withdrawal. Many people who have loving families and no financial worries or stress of any kind feel guilty about being so 'down'.

Withdrawal blues do not single out people with life problems: many people have a temporary 'down'. Sometimes the depressive symptoms are delayed and appear when the sufferers feel they are coping well. Try not to get discouraged if this happens – it will pass. If it gets too much for you to cope with, your doctor may want to give you an antidepressant drug for a short time. Many find this a help, but realize it is a temporary measure. Gradual reduction from these drugs is advisable.

WHAT IS DEPRESSION?

Depression is an illness of the emotions. If it is severe you may feel despair and be so lacking in energy that you cannot get out of bed. If it is mild, you might feel life is a drag and be tired but still be able to function. In addition to losing all interest in yourself and the people around you, life seems to have no meaning or worth. There are also physical effects, such as slow movements; headaches; back pain; heavy, aching limbs; feeling bloated, and either being unable to eat or eating compulsively.

This is very much more than an extension of normal sadness, it is an illness and needs to be treated as such. It is damaging and degrading to keep telling the sufferer to 'pull himself together'. He would dearly love to be 'together' but because he is ill does not know where to start.

IS DEPRESSION NECESSARY?

In anxiety, the functions of the body and the mind are speeded up, whereas in depression they are slowed down. Depression often follows anxiety – it forces us to rest. This could be its function.

Although the slowing-down can be useful, if it goes on too long you need to do something about it. In the same way that we can switch off anxiety feelings and become 'unreal', we can also attempt to run away from sad feelings and become emotionally dead. Unfortunately, when we switch off, we also switch off the good feelings that would normally balance our mood.

Because it can creep up on you, slowly anaesthetizing your feelings, many people live with low grade depressions not knowing life can be other than grey and lethargic. You would not accept a numb arm or useless leg – why accept numb feelings?

WITHDRAWAL DEPRESSION

Not only do you have to cope with a change in brain chemistry during withdrawal, you also have to allow years of suppressed emotions to come out. Although this can be painful, it should be welcomed because it is necessary to express old anger and grieve over old losses before you can be totally well. So many people in withdrawal have said: 'I am feeling so much better physically, but I'm crying over things that happened years ago.' Allow it to happen. You will feel a lot lighter.

After withdrawal, so many excited people have said, 'I'm back to being *me* – this was how I was before I was on pills.' Remember that a period of adjustment is often necessary for family members too. Whilst most people are overjoyed to see the sufferer fitter and more confident, some feel threatened by the change. Perhaps they feel safer if their partner is housebound with agoraphobia or does not have the confidence to venture an opinion.

Keep in mind that when the brain chemistry is back to normal, the withdrawal depression will go.

DEPRESSION AFTER TENSION

It is often difficult to escape depression after a period of severe tension. How often have you heard people say that they kept up whilst they were coping with the strain (for example studying for exams or a long visit from a difficult relative) but became very down when they had a chance to relax? Physical exercise and a determined effort to relax during the stressful time could prevent this type of depression.

Perhaps this is the cause of the withdrawal depression. In the early days of withdrawal the body can react to being less sedated by becoming overactive, but it cannot keep this up, so depression follows. The aim is to gain a balance between the two conditions.

OTHER CAUSES OF DEPRESSION

Sad circumstances

It would be unnatural not to be depressed after the death of a loved one, a divorce, losing a job, or any other sad event. The sad person may be anxious, tearful and withdrawn. This phase should be regarded as the resting time when the sufferer is adjusting to the loss. Well-meaning friends often urge the sufferer not to cry. This is a great mistake. 'Permission' to grieve must be given. The pain or the embarrassment of the onlookers should not be considered. If grief is repressed or pushed down ('isn't she brave; she's behaving so normally') it may emerge later as physical or depressive illness.

Depression caused by buried emotions

Some people recover from chronic depression when a therapist uncovers childhood trauma such as rejection or sexual abuse. For many it is enough to accept that their depression comes from 'listening to old scripts' (inappropriate responses to situations because of childhood conditioning) and relying on the approval of others for feelings of self-worth.

How does a depressed person look?

If he is very depressed, he could look round-shouldered with his head bowed or pushed forward like a turtle. He often wears a mask-like expression and moves slowly with shuffling steps. The person with what is called 'smiling depression' is the 'joke a minute' person who tries to hide his pain by being the life and soul of the party.

Perhaps this could be called 'The Clown Syndrome'; smiling mouth but sad eyes.

Some things depressed people say
- I feel so isolated, even in a room full of people; I have no interest in anything.
- I know I love my family but cannot *feel* it. I feel they would be better off without me.
- I overreact to anything sad. It's so painful I won't watch the news or read the newspapers. I'm so afraid of seeing anything which makes that pain worse.
- Everyone else looks so normal; it worries me.
- Even the smallest physical task is such an effort. I sit three hours at the breakfast table just staring at the wall.
- I dread a visitor in case I have to make a cup of tea.
- Either I'm too exhausted to talk or I can hear myself gabbling on and on.
- I'm completely preoccupied with myself and my health problems.
- I'm looking for someone to blame and get angry about trivial matters.
- This is just not like me.

How do I cope with the depression?

If your physician has ruled out physical illness, he may want you to have a short course of antidepressant drugs. Careful use of these drugs can for some people have a dramatic effect, but remember they cannot erase bad memories or change the way you feel about yourself. It is your job to express past and present hurts and to take care of yourself, physically and emotionally.

YOU HAVE A CHOICE

You could think of your mind as a cellar. If the door stays closed, old fears and resentments grow like mould. If fresh air is allowed in and the walls are whitewashed, it could be a storehouse for the fruits from the orchard. The decision to open the cellar door may seem hard; it may seem safer to stay depressed. The choice is with you. You can leave all the imprints from the past and the opinions of others behind and, just think of it, you could also leave *guilt* behind: all the things you have been beating yourself with for years, including, 'Why did I take those pills? What a mess I am!' One woman said she felt liberated when she realized she was not guilty. She kept repeating the phrase 'not guilty'. Not guilty of what? She was guilty of no crime nor evil, but had an accumulation of a million minor misdeeds she had scored against herself which served to make her feel perpetually guilty.

WHAT ABOUT YOUR SCORE?

Stop carrying around your parents' expectations, resentments and fears. Does it really matter *now* if your father wanted a boy and you were a girl, that you left the latch off the gate and the dog got hit by a car, that you didn't work in school, that you've got skinny legs, that you did not succeed like your brother, that you don't do your own car maintenance, or that it's six weeks since you washed the kitchen floor? No – none of these things matter. What *does* matter is that you are *you*, you are unique and until you forgive yourself, love yourself and realize your own self-worth, the depression will stubbornly refuse to go. Life is better when you are real. Own your feelings. From childhood we try to please those around us by denying our own feelings, and holding them in with tension. This is the start of neurosis – 'pretend'.

CELEBRATE THE END OF 'PRETEND'

1. Accept full responsibility for your physical and emotional well-being.
2. Stop drifting aimlessly. Decide what you want.
3. Think for yourself. You do not need the permission or confirmation of others before you think or act.
4. Serving others and not recognizing your own needs is not noble; it is foolish because you will resent it in the end.
5. Stop being a 'professional people pleaser'.
6. Stop setting yourself too high a standard to reach and constantly indulging in self-criticism when you cannot maintain it.
7. Acknowledge your talents and capabilities and recognize that everyone is of equal worth.
8. Allow yourself the satisfaction of finishing some task, however menial.
9. Don't compare your efforts with the efforts of others; you do not need to prove your worth by superior performance.
10. Acknowledge that no one can insult you or put you down unless you accept his or her authority over you.
11. Concentrate on the good things about yourself.
12. Recognize your need for a good diet, fresh air, sleep, relaxation, rewarding work and companionship.
13. Beware of self-pity.
14. Behave towards yourself as you would towards someone you love.
15. Allow others to care for you.

BE PATIENT – IT WILL GO

Don't be discouraged if you feel you are following all the rules and are still not improving. It takes time. You may feel very negative about your progress, but others may have noticed encouraging little signs in you.

Things People Say When They Are Moving Forward
- For the first time I could feel the effect my depression was having on those around me.
- My facial muscles felt strange – then I realized I was smiling at a baby.
- My first thought when I woke up was about a cup of coffee, not about struggling through the day.
- I bought a packet of seeds and realized for the first time I was thinking beyond the gloomy moment.
- I was half way through the meeting when I found I was interested and not resenting every moment of it.
- I forced myself to tidy the garage and was astonished to find two hours had passed. Time had been passing so slowly.
- I bought a book at the airport and didn't feel irritated when a child dropped ice cream on my shoe. They may seem small things, but I feel really free.

Nature does not heal in a straight line

So many people have said they feel devastated when they go down again after they have felt lighter for a while. This is what happens in natural healing. In time, the lighter periods will get longer and longer and then you will be well. Remember too, that even if you have had a long spell of being well and go down, what you did last time worked – it will work again.

10 *Physical Problems*

CHEST SYMPTOMS

Whilst the major cause of chest symptoms in withdrawal is due to hyperventilation, *all chest problems must be reported to your physician.*

Huge numbers of people have had cardiac investigations (many have been admitted into intensive care) for chest pain, tightness across the chest, palpitations or missed beats, breathing difficulties, numbness or pain down the left arm when they have been reducing their drugs too quickly. Their investigations proved negative and their symptoms abated as withdrawal progressed. For exercises to control hyperventilation (overbreathing) see page 121.

ABDOMINAL SYMPTOMS

Abdominal pain and nausea are often features of drug withdrawal but even if you can date your symptoms from the beginning of withdrawal you should consult your physician.

The colic-type pains and diarrhoea or constipation are usually diagnosed as the 'Irritable Bowel Syndrome'. Many people have full abdominal investigations but the cause of the problem cannot be found. The modern approach to the 'Irritable Bowel Syndrome' seems to be a high fibre diet. There is no doubt that in withdrawal this seems to make matters worse. This is discussed further in the section on the post-withdrawal period on page 76 and also in *Irritable Bowel Syndrome and Diverticulosis – A Self-help plan* by this author, published by Thorsons (1990). Chronic diarrhoea can also be a side-effect of tranquillizer use. There have been several reports of people who have had diarrhoea for years having no more trouble after only a few weeks of complete withdrawal.

Slight bowel incontinence can be a feature of withdrawal. It is temporary.

Urinary symptoms

Frequency, burning and incontinence are reported. Again, investigations usually prove negative. See page 102.

HORMONE IMBALANCE

Tranquillizers affect every system in the body, so it is not surprising that they affect the endocrine system. Thyroid levels can be disturbed and swollen thyroid glands have been reported.

Most of the hormonal symptoms are at their worst when the user is taking the full dose of tranquillizers. They may change during withdrawal, but return to normal when withdrawal is completed. For instance, all interest in sex may be lost whilst taking tranquillizers. The opposite may happen for a time during withdrawal before normality returns.

Some women, who suffered years of heavy periods when they were on pills, find they have a normal flow when they have come through withdrawal. Vaginal discharge, burning vulva, and increased pre-menstrual tension can also cause temporary discomfort.

Research has shown that a hormone called prolactin, which stimulates lactation, is released during tranquillizer therapy. Because of this, breast symptoms are commonly reported. They range from a slight, pale brown discharge to considerable quantities of milk. This has happened up to 16 years after the last pregnancy. After you have been examined by your physician, be patient and the symptoms will go when you are through withdrawal.

Men and breast symptoms

Men get very worried about this; they too, report swollen, tender breasts, and sometimes there is slight discharge. They also complain of impotence, loss of seminal fluid, and pain in the testicles. Often men in their thirties and forties have eruptions of adolescent acne.

When the hormone levels return to normal, all the symptoms will disappear.

INFLUENZA-TYPE SYMPTOMS

If you experience headaches, sore throats, stuffy nose, burning skin etc., it may be that you are cutting down too quickly. Some people realize they have had episodes of this 'influenza' for years – each time they forgot to take their pills. Some had years of ruined holidays because they thought they were going into a relaxed situation and did not need their pills. Many remembered dramatic flu-like illnesses when their pills were stopped during hospitalization for routine surgery. The symptoms always disappeared when they resumed their pills.

MUSCLE PAINS AND SWOLLEN, PAINFUL JOINTS

Aching muscles, spasm and joint pains cause a great deal of distress in withdrawal, but because they are rarely life-threatening symptoms, they are often dismissed as trivial.

Your muscules have to be re-educated. The drugs have artificially relaxed them for so long that they have forgotten how to work efficiently. The stiff, sore heavy limbs will recover, but it is going to take time and care. See page 131.

Jaw pain

If the neck and shoulder muscles are particularly tight, this can contribute to a very painful condition called *trigeminal neuralgia* which is described as a boring pain up through the jaw, usually on one side at a time. It seems at its worst when the sufferer is lying down or taking hot food or drink; sometimes even a light touch on the face is enough to trigger it off. Low blood sugar levels can also encourage this pain. It resembles toothache; and unfortunately, many people in withdrawal have had a full dental clearance, in an attempt to gain relief.

Treating the spasm in the neck and shoulder muscles and normalizing the circulation to the head is the most effective treatment. Some have been helped by wearing a removable plastic shield over their bottom teeth at night to prevent spasm in the jaw. Others found sucking ice, or holding a mouthful of whisky on the affected side helpful.

The people who have suffered this pain are usually those who have withdrawn acutely, and it should not trouble you if you are withdrawing carefully. If, however, you have to withdraw quickly and find this pain too much to cope with, see your physician. Whilst it is better to avoid other medications during withdrawal, if symptomatic relief is necessary, the drug of choice for this pain is Tegretol. Analgesics rarely have much effect. Although your aim is to be drug-free, don't be too disappointed if you occasionally have to take something for a short time.

FEELINGS OF THE GROUND MOVING

Many people say that they feel as if the ground is moving when they walk, or that they are walking on cotton wool. This can be alarming but does settle down as withdrawal progresses. It may be that the area of the brain responsible for co-ordination is temporarily affected.

Ataxia (unsteady walk) can also be experienced in severe anxiety states where there has been no drug involvement.

FEELINGS OF ELECTRICITY, NUMBNESS AND BURNING

Many people complain of tingling all over (but particularly in the hands and feet) and also of feelings like electric shocks going through the body. The cause of the tingling is usually hyperventilation and the feelings of electric shock could be an exaggeration of normal nerve impulses. We are, after all, electrical beings; our muscles, hearts, nerves, etc. all run on electricity. Withdrawal causes such an upheaval in the body that it is bound to upset our electrical circuits. Equilibrium will be restored.

CHANGES IN BODY TEMPERATURE

Some people say they are 'on fire' while others say they feel icy cold or alternate between the two. It is not unusual for the temperature-regulating mechanism to be temporarily disturbed in drug withdrawal.

11 The 'Because' of Withdrawal Symptoms

Disheartened people often ring tranquillizer lines and say: 'I have been so well for months and now I feel awful; my abdomen is bloated and heavy, so many foods seem to upset me, I'm not sleeping again and the depression is coming back.' Don't get discouraged if this has happened to you; there are some answers.

Millions of people worldwide have come through withdrawal from these drugs and regained their health and self-esteem. Many have done it alone in very difficult circumstances. There are some, however, who get 'stuck' and fail to make progress, or who recover for a time and then relapse. At this point many health professionals can only look in one direction – the patient is drug-free; he is still having problems, therefore he is a 'this-or-that personality type' and has deep psychological problems. Withdrawal can act as a catalyst, and therefore there are some people who need a great deal of psychological help, but for others it can be a waste of time. Because of the extremely complicated nature of illness caused by the use of these drugs and the uniqueness of the withdrawal syndrome, the nature of the sufferer's symptoms should be carefully evaluated. All the psychological tricks in the book will not work if the anxiety or depression stems from the *physical* consequences of tranquillizer therapy or the physical results of withdrawal. For example, many people who have not been helped by the psychological approach have recovered when their chronic candidiasis, allergies or thyroid problems have been treated. These conditions are very common both during and after withdrawal. A combination of physical and psychological therapy is often needed, but in my experience, psychological therapy alone is a very long way around the tranquillizer withdrawal problem.

THE POST-WITHDRAWAL PERIOD

Some people do recover very quickly after cessation of these drugs but more usually it takes time, after you have stopped taking the drugs, for the body (particularly the immune system, it seems) and the mind to recover from the ordeal. Many people feel they should be fit and well the moment they are drug-free. This is unrealistic for two reasons: one is that although the drugs may be removed from the bloodstream quite rapidly, the deposits stored in body tissue may take a considerable time to be excreted. This could be the reason why some people report cyclical (usually about six monthly), albeit milder, returns of symptoms they experienced in early withdrawal. It could be that the symptoms are the result of tissue levels of the drug periodically becoming low enough to cause withdrawal feelings, before levelling off again. The sufferer understandably gets dispirited during these 'lows' and needs to be reassured that it is a positive sign; the body is cleaning out the drugs efficiently.

SOME OF THE CAUSES OF POST-WITHDRAWAL PROBLEMS

Vitamin and mineral deficiencies

It is known that these drugs block the absorption of zinc. Since it is unlikely that this mineral is affected in isolation, and it is possible that many vitamins and minerals are malabsorbed during tranquillizer therapy, it is common for people on tranquillizers to have a very poor nutritional profile. For some reason, even if they are eating sensibly, this can become dramatically worse during withdrawal.

Signs of deficiencies regularly noticed

There are many complaints of sore tongues. These can be: swollen, smooth and shiny red, or bright red at the tip. The taste buds can be enlarged. The surface can be deeply fissured or have patches like a map and underneath the veins can be swollen.

- Mouth ulcers, bleeding gums and cracks at the sides of the mouth and recurrent herpes (cold sores) are also frequently seen.
- Spontaneous bruising, falling hair and the slow healing of wounds are other complaints.
- Muscular jerking and cramp are widely reported.

When the body is under stress (which withdrawal, because it is a physical and nervous problem, undoubtedly causes) the daily need for nutrients is dramatically increased. For this reason a healthy diet may not be enough and you could probably speed up your recovery if you take the necessary supplements. The ideal solution is to have some nutritional screening to show where the deficiencies are.

If you cannot find professional help and have to rely on self-help, there are many excellent books around on nutritional medicine. A very popular one is *Nutritional Medicine* by Dr Stephen Davies and Dr Alan Stewart, published by Pan. It is not a good idea to take handfuls of vitamins in the hope that you will find the right ones. There can be pitfalls in taking vitamins indiscriminately; for example, large dosages of vitamin D can be toxic and taking one

B vitamin on its own can deplete your supply of the other B vitamins. People in withdrawal are often very low on the B vitamins (the B status of the nation is generally poor – there would be a lot less tired, sad people around if this was not so) but many find they cannot tolerate a decent dose of B complex – it either upsets their digestion or causes insomnia. A way around this can be to take a small dose of B complex or use it intermittently and use some of the other Bs separately for specific effects. For example B_3 can be a powerful tranquillizer (it was once thought to be the endogenous [made within the body] benzodiazepine). The use of separate B vitamins, usually with calcium, is described in *No More Fears* by Dr Douglas Hunt (see Further Reading).

SUPPLEMENTS WHICH CAN HELP WITHDRAWAL SYMPTOMS

When choosing your supplements include vitamin C, to help your body detoxify, and a balance of calcium and magnesium for the nervous system. Vitamin B complex (try to find a yeast-free product) also helps the nerves. You are likely to be low in zinc not only because of malabsorption but also because zinc is lost in the sweat and you are probably sweating a great deal in withdrawal.

You should not need to take supplements for ever; they should be taken only for the duration suggested, at the recommended dosage. As you recover, a healthy diet should take care of your needs.

Remember that the body may take a week or two to adjust to having its nutritional state changed. Introduce one supplement at a time and increase the dosage gradually, perhaps taking a quarter of the recommended dosage at first. If you start them all at once you will not know which one is upsetting you. Vitamins B and C can have a stimulating effect so it is better to take them after breakfast. If you find that you are developing symptoms such as cystitis, bowel problems or itching around the anus, try another brand. If you find your body in its present state will not tolerate supplements at all, you will have to discover which foods have high proportions of the nutrients you are lacking and increase your intake of these. Try supplements again in a couple of months.

A WORD ABOUT EFAs (ESSENTIAL FATTY ACIDS)

Supplementation with Evening Primrose oil or fish oils has been of great benefit to many people in withdrawal. It helps detoxification, aching joints, the skin, the hormone levels and generally helps the body to regain balance. It needs certain vitamins and minerals for its absorption such as zinc, B_6, B_3 and vitamin E. There is a wealth of information in *Evening Primrose Oil* by Judy Graham (Thorsons, 1984). Your pharmacist should also be able to help you; it is often prescribed for Premenstrual Tension.

TRANQUILLIZERS AND THE IMMUNE SYSTEM

The mushrooming problem of fungal infections

The fungus *Candida albicans* lives in our bodies from infancy in places like the bowel, mouth and vagina and also on the skin. The defence system of the body can normally cope with it at these sites and it is only when we are 'run down' that it can cause infections. Formerly a short course of anti-fungal drugs was usually all that was necessary for this type of infection, but modern living seems to have complicated the picture.

A man-made problem

The reason for the increase in fungal infections over the past three decades seems to be the result of ecological carelessness with both the planet and the human body. The pollution of the planet needs no elaboration, but the pollution of the human body is less widely known, and although the damage done there is more subtle, it is just as sinister. Many medications, substances which purport to restore or maintain health, start the damage; we complete it by our insistence on fuelling our bodies with a diet which at best is unhelpful, and at worst harmful.

Some of the medicines involved in causing this chaos are undoubtedly vital in life-threatening illnesses, but the injudicious use of them can also be life-threatening, or at the very least can cause chronic minor problems that keep people permanently 'below par'. These drugs include antibiotics, contraceptive pills, steroids, and some ulcer medications. Because of widespread reporting both from professionals and lay workers supporting people through withdrawal, tranquillizers and sleeping pills in the Valium group should be added to this list.

Therefore, pollution, some medications and unhealthy diets (those rich in refined carbohydrates and junk foods) all conspire to allow this parasitic yeast to get out of hand. The result is that large numbers of people walk around with a digestive system equal to a gardener's 'grow bag' – a Shangri-La for these nasty little colonizers.

In the gut, the happy Candida live off the fat, or in this case the sugar of the land, have the dark moist conditions they love and are aided and abetted by antibiotics, which kill off their enemies, the good bacteria. The contraceptive pill and steroids seem to act as fertilizers. Although it is unclear why, it has been observed that it is when long-term users of tranquillizers and sleeping pills (the benzodiazepines) are cutting down or stopping their pills that the Candida problems start. Although there can be mild infections in early withdrawal, typically, the most severe problems occur in the post-withdrawal period, often six or twelve months or even longer after complete withdrawal.

As the Candida takes over, the bowel becomes an overactive fermentation tank; a great deal of gas is formed causing abdominal bloating and often an alteration in bowel habits, diarrhoea or constipation.

If this were the whole story it would not be cause for consternation, but unfortunately this is only the beginning. Candida can change from the simple form which causes oral or vaginal thrush to the invasive mycelial fungal form. This more sinister organism grows root-like tendrils which can actually penetrate the wall of its habitat. So instead of being a sealed unit the bowel becomes a leaking pipe through which the waste products of digestion and the poisons manufactured in the 'Candida chemical factory' can escape into the bloodstream, causing widespread problems. The Candida has a perfect transportation system to parts of the body which it does not normally inhabit and where there is no defence system to cope with it. The list of symptoms caused by chronic candidiasis is formidable – a list so long and with so many apparently unrelated symptoms that the only possible explanation would seem to be hypochondriasis.

PSYCHOLOGICAL PROBLEMS

When man in careless mood upsets natural systems and creates new diseases he excels nature. No longer is this a simple yeast causing trouble in tiny mouths and larger vaginas, but a complex organism capable of producing severe physical and psychological illness – psychological illness not of the 'pull yourself together' genre, but a type caused by the waste products of the Candida altering the chemistry of the brain. The resulting symptoms can range from irritability, confusion and hopelessness to severe anxiety, depression, and a schizophrenia-like illness. Food and chemical allergies are frequently seen in people with chronic Candida problems and because the symptoms include depression and anxiety it is often thought to be psychiatric illness.

PHYSICAL PROBLEMS

Infections appear not only at the expected sites, the mouth, skin, vagina, penis and nail-beds, but also through the whole of the digestive tract. So by the time the ears, sinuses, throat and bladder are added, few parts of the body escape. Also, because the forty-plus chemicals produced by the fungus include hormones, the endocrine system can be upset, causing menstrual problems, severe premenstrual tension, impotence and thyroid dysfunction.

CANDIDA SYMPTOMS COMMONLY REPORTED

Fortunately, these symptoms are not as formidable as they appear because they do respond to self-help: discomfort in the abdomen, bloating, gas, wakefulness, constipation/diarrhoea, frequent cystitis which does not respond to antibiotics, vaginal discharge, infection in the penis with soreness and discharge, mouth infections, ear infections (often a watery discharge which makes the skin around the ear sore), depression, anxiety, irritability, poor memory, poor concentration, chronic catarrh. Other problems are nail-bed infections, athlete's foot, scalp problems, sores in the nose, cracks at the side of the mouth, coated sore tongue and inside of cheeks. The soft palate and throat can also be affected. In fact some people say they feel inflamed from the mouth to the anus which becomes sore and itches.

THE IRRITABLE BOWEL SYNDROME

Very large numbers of people on these drugs and in withdrawal have had investigations for gastro-intestinal symptoms. The results are invariably negative and the patient is diagnosed as having 'The Irritable Bowel Syndrome'. This really means 'I cannot discover the cause of your symptoms.' The prescribed treatment, a high-fibre diet, always makes the symptoms worse. This is not surprising; if the cause of the problem is Candida, the diet would include foods to 'feed' the yeast, and if the cause were allergies it would increase the intake of wheat, usually in the form of bran – one of the most common allergens.

Abdominal symptoms commonly reported: discomfort, bloating, gas, wakefulness, change in bowel habits, constipation/diarrhoea.

Always see your physician if you have persistent abdominal symptoms.

If he or she can find nothing wrong (there is no reliable test for Candida overgrowth in the bowel) you may want to read about the anti-Candida diet in the books mentioned below.

URINARY SYMPTOMS IN WITHDRAWAL

Candida could also be the cause of the endless cystitis seen in withdrawal patients. Cultures fail to produce bacteria and the symptoms do not respond to antibiotics. Reports such as: 'I get a sore bladder if I eat sugary foods, citrus fruit, drink wine or take yeast tablets', are very common. Many people have been found to have frank or microscopic haematuria (blood in the urine) – even those without urinary symptoms. This improves with anti-Candida treatment and the avoidance of the offending foods. Vaginal thrush is also an ever-present problem. Dr Patrick Kingsley has written a very helpful book on this subject – *Conquering Cystitis*: A self-help guide to understanding and controlling cystitis – available from Abaco Publishing, P.O. Box 23, Coalville, Leicestershire.

FUNGAL SKIN PROBLEMS

Many people with fungal skin problems have been said to be suffering from nervous rashes. They can appear as dry, scaly red patches appearing anywhere on the body, but more usually over the cheek bones, at the sides of the nose, by the ears and on the hands. Anti-Candida treatment, sunshine and fresh air, anti-dandruff shampoo and anti-fungal creams are used.

FOOD AND CHEMICAL SENSITIVITIES (INTOLERANCE) IN WITHDRAWAL

Hundreds of calls come in about this. People say, 'I was doing so well until this started.'

Food and chemical intolerances often accompany Candida. Symptoms can be: palpitations, flushing, headaches, light-headedness, abdominal bloating or breathlessness after being near petrol fumes, gas fires etc.

There are lots of helpful books around which would help you discover which foods are causing your problems and how to rid your home of unnecessary chemicals. Your doctor may be able to arrange some allergy testing.

BRAIN SYMPTOMS

Because chronic candidiasis can produce so many symptoms, including anxiety and depression, it is often diagnosed as psycho-somatic illness. Treatment for 'nerves' does not work but killing off the Candida and restoring the nutritional balance does.

GIVING THE CANDIDA
A HARD TIME

If your symptoms are severe it is advisable to see your physician or a doctor who specializes in clinical ecology. However, because medical recognition of chronic candidiasis is still in its infancy, many people have to rely on self-help treatment. Fortunately this is safe and effective, although it may take many months. The treatment consists not only of killing the Candida with non-drug, anti-fungal agents, such as garlic or substances from the coconut or castor bean oil, but also by transforming the habitat of the Candida from Shangri-La to the Sahara desert. To achieve this, the bowel is kept as clean as possible and re-colonized with good bacteria such as *Lactobacillus acidophilus* which is available in live yogurt or in some health supplements. In addition, olive oil and yeast-free minerals and vitamins are taken to strengthen the immune system. This further discourages Candida growth; as does a healthy diet low in refined carbohydrate and yeast-containing foods. When fresh air, sunlight, adequate rest and exercise are added, this rogue yeast has to retreat with its tendrils between its legs.

TREATMENT

There are anti-fungal drugs, but the non-drug preparations seem just as effective and have fewer side-effects. Some people have controlled their Candida problems by taking fresh garlic. This is not only anti-fungal and anti-bacterial (and alas, anti-social) but it also lowers the cholesterol level and helps to detoxify the body. Many have said it also helped the depression and increased energy levels.

Build up to three cloves daily. Crush it, mix with milk or yogurt and pour it down like medicine; don't linger over it. You may need several glasses of water to wash it down. It can make you feel nauseated at first but this does not last long and subsequently you will feel a pleasant warmth inside. If you cannot cope with the taste or your friends cannot stand the smell, look for a commercial garlic preparation in pill or capsule form which still contains allicin, the anti-fungal agent, which can be lost in some manufacturing processes. If you cannot tolerate foods in the onion family, you could try one of the other preparations. If your local health food shop cannot help you could write to Green Farm (see page 166).

SPREADING THE WORD

The work of American doctors C. Orion Truss M.D. and William G. Crook M.D. has been valuable in alerting both professionals and the public to the problem, but how long will it be before their pioneering efforts are universally accepted? Until 'Candida consciousness' is raised, not only are sufferers from the more severe mental and physical manifestations of chronic candidiasis going to be misdiagnosed and inappropriately treated, but also sufferers from infections (for example, of the bladder, ears, and skin) thought to be bacterial in origin, are going to have their conditions aggravated by antibiotics and steroids.

MISDIAGNOSED ALLERGIES AND CANDIDA

Here are some case histories to illustrate this:

Jennifer had been off Valium for nine months. She was pleased with her progress until she developed a persistent infection in her right ear. There was a watery discharge from her ear which infected the surrounding skin. After several months and three different courses of antibiotics a culture was sent to the laboratory. It confirmed a fungal infection which cleared up quickly with anti-fungal treatment.

Paula's story is more dramatic and shows how undetected

allergies can lead to years of ill-health. It also shows how inappropriate treatment compounds the problem.

Her troubles began during pregnancy when she lost weight and her bowel habits changed; she was either very constipated or had diarrhoea. After the birth of her son she was covered in a skin rash which sometimes formed blisters. The bowel problems continued and she fainted regularly. She was diagnosed as having post-natal depression and was given tranquillizers. There was no improvement in her condition. She mentioned several times that she was worse after certain foods. Another tranquillizer was prescribed and then an antidepressant but it seemed that the more drugs she took the more depressed she became.

It was suggested that she should be admitted to a psychiatric clinic. She refused this and struggled to exist for the next nine years. Her doctor dismissed her as 'neurotic' and kept looking for non-existent domestic problems. Fortunately, (because this started her detective trail) she developed migraine. The attacks were severe, her sight was affected and she vomited copiously. More pills were prescribed but without effect. This drove her to the library for a book on migraine. There was not a lot of information around in those days about food intolerance but she found a reference to it and for the first time things began to make sense. She adjusted her diet and things seemed to be improving when she had an asthma attack. This had not happened before and she thought she had a chest infection. It was not until she had an identical attack some days later that she made the connection; on both occasions she had drunk a can of orange mineral water. On the second occasion she also had a rash and swollen legs. Her doctor referred her to a gastroenterologist who agreed she had allergy problems. The hospital dietician was kind but appeared to know little about food intolerance.

The breakthrough finally came when she saw the address of an allergy self-help group in a magazine. This led her to a doctor specializing in clinical ecology. She was given anti-fungal drugs and a strict rotation diet. After three weeks she began to feel some improvement and after six months the depression had gone, she was having normal bowel movements and was enjoying her food for the first time for years.

For further reading on this subject:

Candida Albicans: Could Yeast Be Your Problem? Leon Chaitow (Thorsons, 1985)

The Yeast Connection William G. Crook M.D. (Professional Books/Future Health, Inc. P.O. Box 3246, Jackson, Tennessee 38303-0846 U.S.A. Price $11 including postage).

The Yeast Connection Cookbook William G. Crook, M.D. and Marjory Hurt Jones, B.S., R.N. (above address, $15 including postage).

The International Health Foundation maintains a list of physicians and support groups throughout the world. People seeking help on yeast-related problems can write for information to the above address, enclosing a $5 donation.

The Missing Diagnosis, C. Orion Truss M.D. (P.O. Box 26508, Birmingham, Alabama 35226 U.S.A. Price $10).

Coping with Anxiety and Depression (particularly the section on 'Other Causes of Nervous Illness') Shirley Trickett (Sheldon Press, 1989).

12 *Other Causes of Lack of Progress*

Some of the physical causes that hinder recovery have been discussed and if you are not troubled by these but are still unwell, perhaps you are making some of the mistakes discussed below.

RUSHING AROUND LIKE A PAPER KITE

Many people, because they feel well for the first time for years, simply do too much; they get so absorbed in working again they forego relaxation and fresh air; they neglect their diet and then wonder why they feel ill. They cry, 'I'm anxious and aching all over; it's like withdrawal all over again.' Of course it is. If the nervous system is strained, it complains – and remember it will take several years after withdrawal before you can abuse your nervous system the way you used to. The lesson you have had should have been painful enough for you never to risk over-stimulated nerves again.

MISTAKING HYPERACTIVITY FOR BEING WELL

Some people when they are in the hyperactive phase mistakenly think they are well because in spite of getting very little sleep, they have boundless energy. Activity can only be said to be healthy when your muscles respond with fatigue and recover with rest. The hyperactive person does not feel the need for rest; the body responds with exhaustion including frayed nerves.

HANGING ON TO YOUR ANXIETY/DEPRESSION

The responsibility for your emotional state is yours. Outside factors may make life very hard for you, but what actually goes on in your body is determined by *you*; you respond to life with tension, this causes anxiety which in turn causes depression. This is not being done *to* you – you are doing it and, what is more, it is a habit that needs a great deal of determination to break. It is true that during withdrawal the tension is increased because of a chemical reaction and certainly you will need help and support then, but subsequently it is up to you to train yourself to live without tension.

REFUSING TO LOOK AT THE PSYCHOLOGICAL SIDE

Not everyone who takes tranquillizers has deep emotional problems, but those who have and fail to acknowledge it can delay their recovery. Withdrawal often acts as a catalyst; all the stored rubbish from the unconscious is unearthed because the person is too weak to hold it in. This does not happen to everyone because some people are able to express their emotions as they experience them. There are some people, however, who see withdrawal as a totally physical experience and stubbornly refuse to acknowledge that there could be psychological problems too. Hanging on to guilt, anger, frustration and failure to forgive will keep you firmly on the tension, anxiety, depression trail.

USING ILLNESS TO MANIPULATE RELATIONSHIPS

Some people are afraid (albeit subconsciously) of losing love or power if they become well. For example, people may get a great deal more attention, be safe from anger and feel secure in the knowledge that their partner will not leave them if they are sick. Sometimes a person will also stay sick to punish a partner for old misdeeds.

LACK OF EXERCISE

Are you holding yourself back with tension because you are too afraid to really move? You need to take this really seriously. Anxiety, depression and aching muscles will not go until you do. Build up an exercise programme gradually until you are doing really tiring exercise at least three times weekly. If you have physical problems other than withdrawal problems, consult your doctor about how much exercise you should attempt.

YOU HAVEN'T A CHANCE

If you don't follow the rules (good nutrition, exercise, accepting the past etc); if you drink alcohol excessively, smoke, and refuse to control tension, you can forget it, you will not recover.

13 Withdrawal and Other Medications

Because they are having a bad time with tranquillizers many people become worried about all medications; in fact some people become pill-phobics. They suffer back pain, raging toothache and other miseries rather than take a couple of painkillers. The stress caused by the pain would probably be as injurious to the body as the pills. Some self-help groups foster this attitude and unfortunately, lose a few customers on the way; people who have previously failed to withdraw from tranquillizers have succeeded subsequently when they have had short-term or intermittent relief from other drugs; for example, the use of a non-benzodiazepine sedative every third night for someone who has severe insomnia can be the difference between success and failure.

QUERIES ABOUT DRUG INTOLERANCE

Question: I have made several attempts to take medications my doctor has prescribed to ease withdrawal symptoms but my body seems to object strongly. Do other people say this?

Answer: Yes they do, in their hundreds. Perhaps your body (particularly your liver) is trying so hard to clean out the other drugs it refuses to accept any more at the moment. Some people have said they became jaundiced when they tried other medications.

QUESTIONS AND ANSWERS ABOUT ANTIDEPRESSANTS

Question: I was prescribed tranquillizers five months ago because I was anxious about my financial affairs and could not sleep. My business is improving and I feel calmer, but I get very depressed. I have not had this before; is it the tablets or do I need antidepressants?

Answer: Tranquillizers are downers and depression is the most common side-effect. You must always see your doctor if you are severely depressed, but it sounds as though the answer for you could be slow withdrawal from the tranquillizers and taking care of your general health.

Question: I have been on tranquillizers and antidepressants for years; I am coming off the tranquillizers. Should I reduce the antidepressants at the same time?

Answer: It could be better to wait until you are through tranquillizer withdrawal and feel settled. Then check with your doctor before slowly reducing the antidepressants.

Question: Why do I have to do it slowly? Will I have withdrawal symptoms from these too?

Answer: Some people do have a withdrawal reaction. It can
                   be minimized by a gradual withdrawal; this is also
                   a precaution against rebound depression, which
                   can be a feature particularly after long-term use.

Question: I have never been on tranquillizers, only anti-
                   depressants. I am cutting them down and I feel so
                   ill. Am I imagining this?

Answer: No, you are not imagining this. It is well-
                   documented that anxiety, insomnia and other
                   problems can be experienced when these drugs are
                   stopped (see Further Reading – The British Medi-
                   cal Association's Guide to Medicine and Drugs).
                       Withdrawal reactions from antidepressants are
                   common and can closely resemble tranquillizer
                   withdrawal, although it does not seem to take so
                   long. Just follow the rules for tranquillizer with-
                   drawal.

Question: I have been off tranquillizers for a year, and now
                   I am coming off antidepressants. I feel I have gone
                   back to square one. Is this new withdrawal, or have
                   the antidepressants been covering up the tran-
                   quillizer withdrawal symptoms?

Answer: It is often difficult to say, but it is more likely to be
                   withdrawal from the antidepressants causing the
                   symptoms. It is hard on you having to cope with
                   this twice, but it is well worth it, keep going.

Question: I have been on tranquillizers and antidepressants
                   for many years. Since I have come off tranquil-
                   lizers, the antidepressants seem to make me feel
                   very 'high'. Is this right?

Answer: This can happen; when the sedating effect of the tranquillizers is removed, the stimulating effect of the antidepressants is often too much. This is particularly likely if you have been on them a long time. What usually happens is that the antidepressant is either cut down or withdrawn completely (in stages). This has worked well for some people; others have found a change of antidepressant effective.

Question: My doctor has been very helpful during withdrawal but now he wants me to take antidepressants. I have tried, but they make me feel so ill.

Answer: Your body is just getting rid of one chemical; perhaps it won't accept another. If you are not severely depressed keep going without them, but do remember to exercise as much as possible.

Whilst the aim is to be drug-free, sometimes temporary relief of the symptoms is necessary. People who feel suicidally depressed do not have a choice. Antidepressant drugs have been very effective for some; they have had a short course which balances their mood and then they have tapered them off.

Question: Do some people come off their tranquillizers and stay on the antidepressants?

Answer: Yes, this is common. Some people who have been on both long-term say they feel better being off the tranquillizers but they cannot manage without a maintenance dose of antidepressants.

If this is your experience try not to feel a second-class citizen because you are still on some medication. If you feel well on them and are not putting on weight, feeling over-stimulated, oversedated, or suffering any other side-effects, take good care of your general health and relax.

BETA BLOCKERS

If your doctor has prescribed these drugs for reasons *other* than to ease the withdrawal symptoms; for example, for high blood pressure or heart trouble, you must continue to take them as instructed.

Reactions to taking them for withdrawal symptoms vary; some people find it helpful to take a small dose when they feel panicky, others take them three or four times daily for weeks or months. There are however some disadvantages in doing this. A sizable proportion of those who have taken them regularly say they are less anxious on them but the benefits are outweighed by the side-effects; depression, nausea, retention of fluid, and also many people have trouble coming off these drugs after continuous use. Severe anxiety, puffy faces, swollen joints and rashes have been reported.

CAUTION

If you take these drugs continuously, withdrawal must be tapered. Follow the instructions of your doctor.

ANTIBIOTICS

It is not surprising that there are complaints of depression and digestive upsets from people who have needed antibiotics during withdrawal: this happens to some people who have not had other drugs. If you have an infection that has failed to respond to natural healing methods such as garlic, fluids and rest you may need to take an antibiotic. What you can do is minimize trouble by replacing the good bacteria in the bowel which are being killed off by the drug. You can do this by eating live yogurt or finding a supplement in your health store which contains *Lactobacillus acidophilus* (see page 85). If you have been on them long-term you may also need to take a yeast-free vitamin B complex formula.

CAUTION
1. You may risk severe illness if you have a serious infection and refuse antibiotics.
2. You may now be allergic to an antibiotic you were formerly able to tolerate.

MAJOR TRANQUILLIZERS (CHLORPROMAZINE)

In general these drugs are used for the more severe psychiatric illnesses. Undeniably they have side-effects, but they do improve the quality of life for many seriously ill people. Withdrawal from these drugs must always be under careful medical supervision, except perhaps in the instances below:

1. Where a small dose of a major tranquillizer has been prescribed, for example for life trauma. More and more doctors are doing this because of the worries about the benzodiazepines.
2. Where major tranquillizers have been used to cover withdrawal from tranquillizers in the Valium group.

It is unwise to do this because the eventual withdrawal from the major tranquillizers can be just as difficult as the withdrawal from minor tranquillizers, and from the perspective of finding medical help, much more difficult. The difficulties of withdrawing from benzodiazepines are well documented, and public and medical awareness continues to grow. This is not so with the major tranquillizers and many doctors do not recognize that there can be similar problems when these drugs are withdrawn, particularly if it is done too rapily. The other worry is that the side-effects of the major tranquillizers can be much more serious than those experienced during benzodiazepine therapy.

CAUTION

1. Do not reduce or stop these drugs without the consent of your doctor.
2. Support groups should have written consent from the physician before agreeing to support a patient through withdrawal from major tranquillizers.
3. Consider carefully before you accept these drugs to cover symptoms caused by the withdrawal of tranquillizers or sleeping pills.

ANTIHISTAMINES (AVOMINE, PHENERGAN, SOMINEX)

These drugs are often used for insomnia in withdrawal. They are quite effective although they can make you feel rather jaded in the mornings. They take a long time to act with some people and therefore should be taken early in the evening.

Piriton (Chlorpheniramine)

Can be bought over the counter. It has helped some people to sleep. Others have used it for itching, rashes or a small dose half an hour before meals for food intolerance.

Side-effects:
There do not seem to be any major problems but bloating, constipation and restless legs are reported.

TAGAMET (CIMETIDINE, RANITIDINE)

This drug has been a breakthrough in the treatment of gastric ulcers and has saved countless people from the surgeon's knife. It would seem, however, that because the drug has been around for some time, because it is useful, and because it does not seem to have any serious side-effects, a complacency towards it has developed. People are being left on it far too long, month after month, year after year, without any review. A conscientious medical practitioner would be shocked at this, but this is the reality of the situation. It is not surprising that there are increasing calls about this group of drugs.

When the familiar gastro-intestinal problems of the post-withdrawal period appear, Tagamet is often prescribed and when the dosage is reduced or stopped distressed callers say: 'I feel so ill – it feels very much like withdrawal again.' The complaints are of anxiety, depression, headaches and nausea. Curiously, several people have said the constipation and colic they experienced during Tagamet therapy disappeared within a few days of withdrawal, no matter how long-standing it had been. It could be argued that because callers had already experienced withdrawal they had an expectation of symptoms when they reduced any medication, but this cannot be so because some of the callers had no previous drug history and knew nothing of tranquillizer withdrawal. Also if people had withdrawal neurosis, they would give the same symptom picture; they don't do this and usually highlight only the symptoms mentioned earlier.

CAUTION
1. These drugs increase the potency of the benzodiazepines.
2. Anecdotal evidence (UK & USA) suggests that they can cause dependence. Withdrawal reactions have been reported.
3. Post-withdrawal fungal infections have been reported.

STEMETIL
(PROCHLORPERAZINE)

These are prescribed in withdrawal for vertigo and also as a mild sedative. The sedative action is not impressive but they do seem to help the vertigo.

Side-effects:
The same as major tranquillizers.

ANTI-INFLAMMATORY DRUGS

During withdrawal these drugs are not well tolerated. They are prescribed for the joint pains. These do ease as withdrawal progresses so you might be better trying natural methods including a colon cleansing diet, food rotation (for food intolerance), fish oil, or Evening Primrose oil and water therapy (page 79). Many people have benefited considerably from this approach.

STEROIDS

These are occasionally used if the post-withdrawal bowel problem is severe, but more often in a cream for misdiagnosed fungal skin infections, there are however frequent calls from people saying they have been reading about tranquillizer withdrawal and they had suffered the same after withdrawing from the long-term use of steroids.

BARBITURATES

These drugs have a very bad reputation for their abuse potential and because it is easy to fatally overdose on them. They are rarely used. It is a pity that the baby has been thrown out with the bath water, because used with care, they can be extremely helpful in benzodiazepine withdrawal. For example, they can be used intermittently, or for up to six weeks, as night sedation. Insomnia holds many people back and a short break from it can be very helpful.

Of the people who have been given barbiturates for tranquillizer withdrawal problems, both in hospital and in the community, none have developed a new dependence. If you are desperate for sleep perhaps your doctor would give you a prescription where you could be dispensed a two-day supply at a time.

CONCLUSION

Of course it is better to be drug-free as soon as possible, but if you have to take drugs for symptomatic relief in order to achieve this *do not worry about it* as long as it is for short periods and you bear in mind:

ALL SUBSTANCES WHICH SEDATE OR STIMULATE THE NERVOUS SYSTEM ARE POTENTIALLY DRUGS OF ADDICTION.

14 Investigations for Withdrawal Symptoms

In the summer of 1984 the annual report of a lay tranquillizer support group was published in the magazine of a London psychiatric hospital as an example of the work that was being done in the community. Here is the section which refers to investigations for withdrawal symptoms:

THE BETHLAM & MAUDSLEY GAZETTE – SUMMER '84 VOL. 31

Until it emerged that so many long-term users had undergone the same investigations, questions on this were not asked. (The numbers will be for only part of the year.) The symptoms investigated were not associated with drugs either by doctor or patient.

Abdominal
Barium investigations for abdominal pain or chronic diarrhoea. A few had explorative surgery. The Irritable Bowel Syndrome was usually diagnosed. Three who had gastroscopies were found to have severe inflammation.

Urinary
Investigations for urinary tract infection, incontinence, haema-

turia. No organism found – symptoms persisted after Septrin, etc.

Neurological

Five people were investigated for MS (multiple sclerosis). Tests were negative in four. Six people had brain scans for suspected cerebral tumour. All the results were negative. One woman was said to have a degenerative muscular and nervous disease of unknown origin. She is recovering as withdrawal progresses.

Hormonal

Menorrhagia (heavy periods) was commonly reported. This lessened as the dose was reduced and usually cleared completely after withdrawal. Some had already had hysterectomies for this. Six were under thirty years of age.

Breast symptoms: there were several reports of swollen breasts with discharge or even copious lactation. In no case was this associated with childbirth. In the five women who were investigated for suspected tumour on the pituitary, it was between three and six years since the confinement. All investigations were negative. The investigations had been done some years before in some. Drugs were not mentioned as a possible cause of symptoms in any case.

One woman had undergone surgery for the removal of milk ducts. In others, symptoms disappeared as withdrawal progressed.

Part II SELF-HELP TRANQUILLIZER WITHDRAWAL PROGRAMME

15 Detoxification (Excreting the Poison)

WATER INSIDE AND OUT

Keeping the organs of excretion – the bowel, bladder and skin – in good order is essential; unless your doctor has advised a restriction in fluid intake, drink lots of water. It prevents constipation and helps to flush out the drugs; about two quarts daily would be ideal. Diet is also important in the cleansing process. The enzymes in raw vegetables and fruit help to clean your body at a cellular level and also boost energy levels. If you have digestive problems you might be surprised to find that you can digest well-masticated raw vegetables better than cooked ones. This has been a common experience. Leslie and Susannah Kenton's marvellous book, *Raw Energy* (Century Arrow, 1986) is full of exciting research about raw vegetables and fruit.

HOW A TOXIC BOWEL CAN DELAY RECOVERY

The effect of tranquillizers on the bowel is uncertain but there is no doubt that some people suffer temporary damage to the bowel as a result of taking them. Whilst some say that the bowel problems they had suffered from for years, such as chronic diarrhoea, cleared up within two weeks of coming off the drugs, others did not have trouble until they began to withdraw; this is the most usual. If the bowel troubles are not treated they can persist for months or even years after withdrawal. The symptoms are: bloating, abdominal pain, excessive wind, wakefulness, loss of appetite, or eating frequently to try to 'move things along', constipation, diarrhoea or alternate bouts of both, and discomfort after certain foods. People seeking medical help for abdominal symptoms in withdrawal are invariably diagnosed as having either the Irritable Bowel Syndrome or diverticulosis (or diverticulitis). Candida and food intolerance have been discussed elsewhere. Here, a section from *Irritable Bowel Syndrome and Diverticulosis - A Self-help plan* (Thorsons, 1990) has been included.

THE BOWEL AS A DUMPING GROUND

Some people treat their digestive tract like a rubbish disposal system and give little thought to the damage caused by a careless diet. When the colon is irritated by diet, stress, drugs, chemicals and so on, it tries to protect itself by producing more mucus; this can bind with the sludge from refined foods, such as white flour, and build up on the wall of the bowel the way silt builds up in a river. This layer of gluey hardened faeces can weigh several pounds and is a good place for harmful organisms to breed. It also prevents the complete absorption of nutrients by preventing digested food coming into contact with the lining of the bowel. The production of *digestive enzymes*, chemicals necessary to break down the food for complete absorption, is also affected.

HOW DOES A DIRTY COLON AFFECT THE BODY?

The local effects of this poisonous residue are irritation and inflammation. The general effects include: diarrhoea, constipation, fatigue, headaches, dull eyes, poor skin, spots, aching muscles, joint pains and depression. This is because the poisons go through a network of vessels called the lymphatic system to all parts of the body; the equivalent of dirty dish-water is carried around the body, instead of a clean, nourishing fluid, the function of which should be to feed cells not served by blood vessels. The lymphatic fluid also kills off harmful organisms and carries away the refuse.

If the body has to battle against these poisons long-term, it is not surprising that it sometimes has to give up and the disease process takes over: the result – inflammation, infection and degeneration. It is understandable that there are more and more people referred to hospitals for Irritable Bowel Syndrome, colitis (inflammation of the colon), Crohn's disease (inflammation of the small intestine), colon cancer and diverticulitis.

DIVERTICULOSIS

When the muscles of the colon wall have to work overtime to deal with hard stools or lack of bulk in the diet they become weakened and lose their elasticity. This causes pouches called *diverticula* to form and then the condition is known as diverticulosis. The food trapped in these pockets makes wonderful breeding ground for bacteria. The result can be diverticulitis, an infection where there is often a fever and acute abdominal pain. This condition needs medical help.

DIVERTICULA DISEASE/IRRITABLE BOWEL SYNDROME

Where symptoms are not severe and are treated by the GP these two diagnoses are often interchangeable. Men are more likely to be told they have diverticula problems, women are more likely to be told they have Irritable Bowel Syndrome.

CAUTION
If you have abdominal symptoms, even if you feel they date from the beginning of withdrawal, consult your doctor, and only after you have been diagnosed as having the Irritable Bowel Syndrome or diverticulosis should self-help methods be used.

SOOTHING THE BOWEL

You might have to experiment before you find the right treatment for your bowel. These are the things people have found helpful: Taking linseed (1 teaspoonful three times daily or building up to two dessertspoonfuls at breakfast – either in yogurt, on cereals or just chewed throughout the day). Drink water after it and a soothing, cleansing jelly will form in the bowel. Alfalfa tablets or capsules from the health food shop also help to heal the lining of the bowel. *Isogel* is a bulking agent which can be helpful. If you are constipated take it with lots of water; if you have diarrhoea take it with only enough water to get it down. Avoid wheat-based bulking agents. Although because of withdrawal you may not be making essential nutrients, including enzymes, necessary for digestion some of the trouble might be due to over-stimulated nerves. So it is possible that the symptoms will not finally go until your nervous system is in a better state. Slow down, take time and eat slowly, chewing each mouthful very well. Good digestion starts with the food being chemically broken down in the mouth. If you rush your meals this important first stage of digestion is lost.

SPRING CLEANING THE BOWEL

When they become aware of the dangers of a dirty colon some people become too enthusiastic and embark on drastic colon cleansing programmes which can result in poisons pouring into the bloodstream and although the final result is very beneficial it can make the sufferer feel wretched. The experience of detoxification can resemble migraine – blinding headaches, nausea – or 'flu – aches and pains, fever, exhaustion – and nervous symptoms such as anxiety, panic attacks, irritability, weepiness or even quite profound depression. This can be avoided by taking it slowly; flushing the poisons out a little at a time.

WHERE DO I START?

Simply by cleaning up your diet. Cut down on foods which collect on the walls of the bowel: refined flours, sugar, cakes, biscuits, refined cereals, fatty foods, and increase the foods which act as gentle scouring pads as they go through the gut: vegetables, raw and cooked, fruit, fresh, stewed or dried, whole grains and pulses, seeds and nuts. Every time you reach out for a snack, possibly one which has comforted you since childhood, perhaps a piece of white bread or a doughnut, imagine trying to use it to clean out a sticky bowl, then imagine cleaning out the same bowl with a handful of fibrous raw vegetables or chewy brown rice.

FOOD AND SECURITY

People often become anxious or even aggressive when a change of eating habits is suggested, here are some typical comments:

● But sugar gives me energy; I need it. It always makes me feel better.

Sugar has no nutritional value, it is empty calories. Yes, it can give you energy temporarily but it does more harm than good in the long term – see page 125 on blood sugar levels.

● But I must have some bread, I could never feel full without it;

everybody needs it – it is the staff of life.

Wholemeal bread is very good food but for some people wheat and yeast can be the source of major problems (page 83).

● But I've always missed breakfast, had a sandwich at lunchtime and a big meal in the evening.

This is an unhealthy way to eat, expecting your body to function without fuel during your working hours. It can cause fatigue, tension, irritability and overweight.

● But that's not a proper meal . . .

WHAT IS A PROPER MEAL?

Some people cling to the idea that a nutritious meal must be a mixture of protein and starch, such as steak pie, cabbage, potatoes and gravy, or fish, peas and chips. It not only is unnecessary to eat this way but it can also put a great strain on the digestive system. Research has shown that starch – bread, potatoes, sugar – and protein: meat, fish, eggs and poultry, require different gastric juices for digestion, so if they are eaten together, neither food has the medium necessary to break it down efficiently, digestion is slowed down and gas, bloating and indigestion can result. This is explained fully in *Food Combining for Health: Don't Mix Foods That Fight* by Doris Grant and Jean Joice (Thorsons, 1987). It can be very liberating for you and your digestive system to give up old-fashioned ideas. If your diet is varied it is perfectly sound nutrition to eat nothing but apples or grains or vegetables for a meal as long as you eat enough. Proper meals are adequate amounts of a variety of clean foods.

CLEANING UP THE DIET

Note: Any dietary suggestions contained in this book are only for people who are overweight or the correct weight for their height and build. People who have a diet from their doctor or people who have ever had an eating disorder or severe depression must consult their doctor before changing their eating habits.

How long does it take to clean the colon?

The debris has been collecting for years so it is unlikely you will have a pristine inside in a couple of weeks; it could take months. You will know when things are happening: your skin and eyes will look clearer, your digestion will improve, you will have more energy, and niggling aches and pains which have been around for years will disappear. You could feel mentally better too, less jumpy and more clear-headed.

Some people say it feels like grief having to give up their favourite foods, but at the same time they are so delighted by the change in their appearance they are willing to resist a Big Mac or a bowl of English Toffee icecream.

STAGE ONE

Note: This is a clean-up diet rather than an elimination diet for allergies, but in fact some people have found that after cleansing the bowel if they combine foods carefully they can tolerate foods which had previously caused trouble. Also note you are not going to feel good initially; in fact, as you detoxify you could feel tired and heavy-limbed. Some people experience a furred tongue, nausea and joint pains. This is why cleaning out in stages has been suggested. Try to stay with it: the feelings pass in a few days and remember the worse you feel, the cleaner you are becoming inside.

GETTING STARTED

Think about what you are putting in your mouth: has it been messed about, does it contain chemicals, what has been lost in the processing, how is it packaged . . . do you really want to eat dyes, or munch snacks covered with large quantities of salt to conceal the fact that they have been cooked in rancid fat? *Your body is just not built to cope with this.*

Give up!
1. Regular consumption of junk foods.
2. All cow's milk and cheese (except live yogurt), even for a month; these are the main cause of allergic problems in infants and adults so it makes sense to start here.

This request usually brings cries of protest, 'But how can I live without cheese or milk?' – you can, and will be surprised how quickly the desire for these foods will go. You could substitute goat's or sheep's milk yogurt and cheese. Some people use soya milk for drinking, cooking and making yogurt.

3. Cut down on tea, coffee, chocolate and all soft drinks, see page 116.
4. Cut down on alcohol. Make sure you eat fruit or drink fruit juice at the time you would normally have an alcoholic drink.

Increase 'dredger food'
1. Wholegrains, oats, brown rice, barley, millet, rye

2. Pulses; lentils, beans, peas
3. Fruit and vegetables including sea vegetables (sounds better than seaweed!)
4. Fish, olive oil, sunflower oil
5. Nuts (not peanuts) and seeds
6. Take water, fruit juice, herb teas or coffee substitute at some of your tea breaks.

STAGE TWO

You might be ready for this after a week but if you are still struggling, continue stage one for another week.

1. Cut down on meat, eggs, and poultry.
2. Cut down further on tea, coffee, soft drinks and alcohol.

Increase whole clean foods

More vegetables, fruit and grains as above.

STAGE THREE

On paper this is going to look depressing, but when you are up to stage three you should be used to being deprived – although hearty bowls of lentil and vegetable soup, or baked potatoes with nut butter or yogurt and herbs, curried vegetables and rice or pasta tossed in olive oil with garlic mushrooms and tomatoes is not exactly starvation rations, is it?

Eat only

Whole grains, vegetables, sea vegetables, fruit (fresh or dried), nuts, seeds, olive oil or sunflower oil or products made from any of these if they do not contain additives.

Drink

Water, bottled or filtered if possible, fruit juices, preferably diluted, bancha tea, herb teas, coffee substitutes or if you cannot make it without, one cup of weak tea or filtered coffee per day.

YOUR HARD WORK WILL BE REWARDED

By now you might be ready to rush out for fish and chips to settle your nerves – don't despair and think what you will gain.

A. The bowel will work more efficiently, the absorption sites will be cleared, enzyme production will increase and as a result your bowel should be less irritable.

B. Because you have eaten less concentrated protein you will have been eating better combinations of foods. Also, your kidneys and liver will have been rested.

C. Because of reducing your sugar intake, your pancreas will be less strained and your blood sugar levels should be more stable.

D. You will probably have lost some excess weight or puffiness.

E. You will look healthier.

GETTING BACK TO A NORMAL DIET

Introduce foods one at a time and notice if you feel uncomfortable or down with any of them, or if any symptoms such as aching joints, a stuffy nose or headaches reappear. If this happens, restrict the offending food to once every four days.

STIMULATING THE SKIN TO GET RID OF POISONS

Whilst the digestive tract and the kidneys are the main organs of excretion the skin has also a very important part to play; it is a great deal more useful than just a waterproof covering that keeps our bits and pieces together. If it is kept healthy it can be a wonderful waste disposal system. It covers such a large area it is worth getting it to work for you.

Sweating it out
A fever is nature's way of helping us to lose toxins through the skin. You can stimulate sweating with some water therapies.

Water therapy
Regular swimming is very beneficial; steam baths, saunas and jacuzzis also encourage detoxification.

CAUTION
Consult your doctor before using water treatments if you have heart trouble, blood pressure, diabetes, epilepsy or any condition which might be aggravated by extremes of temperature.

Salt baths
These encourage detoxification and greatly help muscle and joint pains. Add 2lb of salt or three cups full of Epsom salts to a comfortably hot bath and lie in it for 20 minutes; add hot water as it cools. If you drink a pint of hot honey and lemon, or peppermint tea whilst you soak it will further encourage sweating. A cold flannel on the forehead might make you feel more comfortable. The next step is to wrap up in cotton towels and get into a warm bed. You should perspire freely and sleep well. If you have to bathe during the day finish with a cold shower and rest for half an hour. You could do this three times weekly.

Foot baths
For aching feet and to stimulate circulation use bowls of hot and cold water alternately, staying two minutes in each; carry on for about twenty minutes. If you wish you could add one cup of salt or ½ cup of Epsom salts to the hot water. When you have finished wrap the feet in a towel and lie down for half an hour.

Skin brushing

This stimulates the lymphatic system and helps the skin get rid of drug residues. It involves brushing all over with a natural bristle brush (dry) for about ten minutes before you shower or bathe. Start with the soles of the feet and work upwards; cover all areas except broken skin, the face, neck and breasts. It can be boring but the results are worth it. In addition to eliminating toxins, it will also improve the texture of your skin, because circulation is increased. Boots and the Body Shop have skin brushes or you might have an old hairbrush that would do the job; wash it carefully. Green Farm have a book on the Toxic Colon and also have skin brushes and herbal colon cleansing preparations. (See page 166.)

Some people found their abdominal symptoms disappeared if they kept to an anti-Candida diet, others found if they kept off dairy produce and wheat (although it was a couple of weeks before they felt any benefit) they improved. Several people found a 70 per cent raw diet worked very well when everything else failed. If you think food intolerance is at the root of your symptoms there are plenty of good books around. *The Complete Guide to Food Allergy and Intolerance* by Dr Jonathan Brostoff and Linda Gamlin (Bloomsbury, 1989) would be a good choice.

Don't forget that persistent diarrhoea does not necessarily mean your colon is clean: a toxic colon could be the cause of the watery stool.

16 Tranquillizers and Over-breathing

Hyperventilation, or over-breathing, is breathing in a rapid, shallow way using the upper chest instead of the abdomen. Breathing in this manner produces more oxygen than the body needs, and the result is a fall in the level of carbon dioxide in the blood. In withdrawal, the central breathing mechanism is temporarily affected. This is why it is important to control over-breathing.

Here is an extract from the *Oxford Textbook of Psychiatry* (1983) which shows how many troubles can come from faulty breathing.

Over-breathing is breathing in a rapid and shallow way which results in a fall in the concentration of carbon dioxide in the blood. The resultant symptoms include dizziness, faintness, numbness and tingling in the hands, feet and face, carpopedal spasms [severe cramp in hands and feet], and precordial discomfort [area of the chest over the heart]. There is also a feeling of breathlessness which may prolong the condition. When a patient has unexplained bodily symptoms, the possibility of persistent over-breathing should always be borne in mind.

BECOME AWARE OF YOUR BREATHING

It may be several weeks before your breathing habits improve, so be patient with yourself.

You might find the following exercises tedious but, as you know, getting better requires effort. If it does not stop you concentrating on the exercises, you could have the radio on. If your heart is bumping away as you lie down you could try closing your eyes and pressing gently on the eyeballs: this causes a reflex slowing of the heart and can be soothing.

If you pull in your abdomen as you breathe in, this restricts the air intake. The aim is to breathe slowly, lifting the abdomen. If you breathe deeply you can become light-headed or your heart may bump a little. This shows how it is not only low carbon dioxide levels but also rapid changes in these levels which can cause symptoms. This is nothing to worry about, and if you get in a muddle take a rest and start again.

HOW DO I KNOW IF I AM OVER-BREATHING?

It is easy to recognize severe hyperventilation: erratic, noisy, rapid breaths where the chest is heaving and the abdomen is barely moving. The person feels the need to take an occasional deep breath and often finds it difficult to breathe out. Hyperventilators sigh a lot.

Chronic over-breathing is not easy to identify because there is nothing dramatic to see or hear – quiet, shallow rapid breaths with most of the movement from the upper chest.

BREATHING EXERCISES

Make the time to do two half-hour sessions daily. If you are having severe symptoms, panic or agoraphobia, a quick five minutes here and there is not enough. The best times are after breakfast and before the evening meal. Sit comfortably in a chair or, better still, lie on the floor or bed, and loosen tight clothing. As you become more skilled, you will be able to practise abdominal breathing anywhere, even standing in a queue.

Slowly and **Gently** Not Deeply and Vigorously

1. Place one hand on your abdomen and one on your chest. The hand on your chest should stay as still as possible. The hand on your abdomen should go up and down as you breathe; visualize a blue and white boat gently rising and falling in the waves.
2. Breathe out through your nose (don't force it), and let your abdomen fall gently as you do so.
3. Breathe in through the nose letting the abdomen rise; make the out breath longer than the in breath.
4. Gradually train yourself to breathe between eight and twelve times per minute. Sometime when you are resting, look at a watch with a second hand and count how many times your chest goes up and down (this is one breath) during half a minute; double it and you will have the rate at which you breathe per minute.

USING BREATHING TO CONTROL PANIC ATTACKS

These can cause a great deal of distress during withdrawal. The sufferer is suddenly overwhelmed by fear for no apparent reason, and often feels that death is not far away. Some people feel unable to move or speak, others shout out for help. Although the attacks usually last only a few minutes it can seem much longer to the sufferer. In a person who is not nervously ill, an exam, or even an exciting social event may produce 'butterflies in the stomach', sweating hands, constriction of the chest, a rise in the heart rate, etc. – all the feelings of raised adrenaline levels. This is a normal response; a panic attack is an exaggeration of this – the cause is an exhausted nervous system. If you are over-enthusiastic the first time you go out jogging, the next day your muscles will complain by being stiff and sore. Panic attacks, agoraphobia, irritability, and many other symptoms are a similar cry for help from your nervous system. It is saying 'Do not abuse me, I have had enough.'

It is often hard to convince someone who is having panic attacks that it is not the onset of some terrible disease. Every symptom – wildly beating heart, rapid breathing, sweating, shaking – is part of the 'fight or flight' response. We do not want to stop this mechanism because we would not survive long without it, but we do want it to stop over-reacting with full-blown panic at every little stimulation.

Primitive humans needed to be able to react like this to escape from dangerous animals. We may need it now to get out of the path of a bus, or a youth on a skateboard! Fear stimulates the chemicals that make us respond quickly. That unpleasant sinking feeling in the abdomen we experience when we are afraid is only a sudden diversion of blood away from internal organs to the legs to allow for greater speed.

The following article shows that one of the major causes of panic attacks is simply not breathing correctly.

'Hyperventilation [shallow breathing] as a Cause of Panic Attacks', Dr Hibbert, British Medical Journal, *Vol 288 28.1.84.*

The syndrome [collection of symptoms] characterised by repeated panic attacks has been known by several names including muscular exhaustion of the heart, neurasthenia [nervous exhaustion], irritable heart, anxiety neurosis, effort syndrome, and cardiac neurosis. The manual's definition of panic disorder states that attacks are manifested by the sudden onset of intense apprehension, fear or terror, often associated with feelings of impending doom. The most common symptoms experienced during an attack are dyspnoea, choking or smothering sensations, dizziness, vertigo, or unsteady feelings, feelings of unreality, paraesthesias [disordered sensation such as tingling and pins and needles] hot and cold flushes, sweating, faintness, trembling or shaking and fear of dying, going crazy or doing something uncontrolled during the attack. Attacks usually last minutes; more rarely hours.

If your attitude is, 'I will die/be sick/faint/wet myself/etc. if I don't fight this panic attack,' you will encourage more attacks. It will be the trigger for stimulating more adrenaline, more fear. If you teach your body to give the correct message to your brain, you can break this chain reaction. More information is given in my book *Coping Successfully with Panic Attacks* (Sheldon Press, 1992).

FIRST AID FOR PANIC ATTACKS

Since the cause of your symptoms is a low level of carbon dioxide, make an effort to retain as much of your own as possible. You can do this by letting out your breath in a long sigh and then cupping your hands around your nose and mouth until you feel better. If you gulp in more oxygen you push out the carbon dioxide, so let your breath out in a long sigh and cup your hands around your nose and mouth to cut down your supply (don't hold your breath). If you are at home you could place a paper bag – never plastic – around your nose and mouth. Do not blow or breathe deeply into the bag, just let the breaths come; they will slow down naturally as you get your own carbon dioxide back from the air in the bag. You can also slow the breathing down by splashing cold water on your face or by putting cold cloths or ice packs over the cheeks and nose. A packet of frozen peas wrapped in a dish towel has often been used with effect.

If breathing is the first thought during panic, what next? The second thought should be: *eat or drink something sweet as soon as possible*. The next chapter explains why this helps and how eating sugar is only a first-aid measure for panic and why it should be followed by a meal and a rest.

17 *Hypoglycaemia (Low Blood Sugar)*

Here is another quote from the annual report of the lay tranquillizer scheme:

HYPOGLYCAEMIA

After the first few weeks of acute withdrawal many described what seemed like hypoglycaemic symptoms. Where gastrointestinal symptoms would allow it, a hypoglycaemic diet helped, particularly where symptoms (including panic attacks) were accompanied by severe hunger. This was a particular problem where there was a high carbohydrate diet and familial diabetes. Several callers who started benzodiazepine therapy between fifteen and twenty-two years of age felt that hypoglycaemic attacks (although this was not suggested at the time) could have been the cause of their original symptoms. Athletic young males seemed most at risk. All felt worse on benzodiazepine therapy. In two, where blood sugar levels were eventually done, they were found to be in the diabetic range after the ingestion of benzodiazepines and below normal when the next dose was due.

Drugs with a short half-life seemed to cause more hypoglycaemia, but all the benzodiazepines seemed to be implicated. In some, symptoms persisted several months after withdrawal.

THE IMPORTANCE OF EATING REGULARLY IN WITHDRAWAL

Addictions and low blood sugar

Many drugs, including alcohol, cigarettes, tranquillizers and sleeping pills, artificially raise the blood sugar levels. When the level of the drug in the blood drops, the blood sugar also falls. There is often a confusion between drug withdrawal symptoms and hypoglycaemic symptoms because they both include headache, anxiety, depression, shaking etc.

Whilst it is difficult to separate the symptoms, it is certainly very clear that people withdrawing from drugs who keep to a low blood sugar eating plan not only dramatically reduce their withdrawal symptoms, but are also much more likely to complete withdrawal and not feel the need to turn to other substances. For example, people withdrawing from alcohol often turn to tranquillizers and vice versa.

Low blood sugar

Hypoglycaemia or low blood sugar is an abnormally low level of glucose in the blood. The food we eat is turned into glucose by the digestive system and we use the energy it produces to nourish our bodies, rather like putting petrol in a car.

Some people think if they eat lots of sugary foods they will be full of energy and the level of glucose (sugar) in their blood will stay normal. This chapter will show that in fact the opposite is true and that it is essential for some people in withdrawal to cut down on these foods.

Hypoglycaemia could be said to be the opposite to diabetes, a disorder where the organ called the pancreas fails to produce the chemical called insulin. Insulin enables us to burn the food we eat to produce energy. The reverse is so in hypoglycaemia. The pancreas is over-stimulated, usually because of nervous exhaustion, and produces too much insulin. This causes the food we eat to be burned up too quickly and we cannot maintain the levels of blood glucose necessary to function normally.

The results are a lot of unpleasant physical effects such as a rapid heartbeat, feeling faint and (because the brain cannot store glucose), there are also unpleasant brain effects such as anxiety, depression, panic attacks and neurotic behaviour.

If you eat sugary foods, particularly when you are very hungry, the pancreas, which is already jittery and in top gear, pushes out more insulin than is necessary to cope with the sugar. The result is a rapid drop in blood sugar levels, and as we have seen the result is a flood of adrenaline.

Cigarettes, caffeine, alcohol in withdrawal

Most smokers seem to smoke more in withdrawal although some stop because of the metallic taste in their mouths. It is probably not the time for you to attempt to give up but try not to chain-smoke or smoke before food; this will make you very jittery. Cut down on tea and coffee too and have it very weak. Most people have said alcohol makes the symptoms very much worse, others have used it to help them to sleep. This should be regarded as a temporary help because of the danger of another dependence.

Familial history

It is very important for people in withdrawal who are from families where there are other low blood sugar problems (asthma, arthritis, allergy etc.) to follow the hypoglycaemic eating plan. It is also wise to start the diet three or four weeks *before* you intend to stop smoking or drinking or before you cut down on tranquillizers or sleeping pills.

EATING PLAN TO KEEP BLOOD SUGAR LEVELS STABLE

If your doctor has already given you a diet to follow consult him or her before you make any changes in your eating pattern.

Principles of the diet

The aim is to avoid foods and substances that are quickly absorbed in order to minimize rapid changes of the level of glucose in the blood.

Avoid or cut down to a minimum: refined carbohydrates

Sugar, sweets, chocolate, white bread, white flour, cakes, cookies, pastry, alcohol, sweet drinks, junk foods.

Eat: non-refined carbohydrates

Non-refined carbohydrates (complex): wholegrain cereals, wheat, oats, barley, rice, rye, millet.

Give up processed breakfast cereals and make your own muesli from whole oats, nuts, seeds (sunflower, pumpkin or sesame are all very nutritious) and a little dried fruit — sultanas, apricots etc. If you are used to eating 'plastic bread' you will love the taste of wholegrain brown bread. If you normally eat brown bread make sure it is wholegrain.

Eat: protein

Animal protein: meat, fish, poultry, cheese, eggs, milk, yogurt.
Vegetable protein: nuts, seeds, peas, beans, lentils and possibly small amounts in all vegetables.

There is always a lot of argument about how much protein should be included in any diet. The early diets for low blood sugar were very high in protein. Eating this way certainly controls the blood sugar but more recent research has shown that the body does not like too much concentrated protein and blood sugar levels can be kept steady on smaller amounts particularly if lots of raw vegetables are included.

Eat large quantities of vegetables

These will supply you with essential minerals and vitamins and provide fibre (roughage). Some people have become over-anxious about fibre: bran with everything. This is not a good idea: it can irritate the bowel and hinder the absorption of some minerals. Eating vegetables is a better way to get fibre.

Eat lots of fresh fruit

Although fruit contains quite a lot of sugar, it is in a different form (fructose); it does not need insulin for its digestion; therefore, it is an ideal food to help slow down the pancreas.

Eat some fat

People tend to concentrate on low fat (often dangerously low) diets and think this will take care of all cholesterol problems. There are other factors just as important: stress, and a diet low in raw vegetables and fruit, can be just as damaging as moderate amounts of butter. Also remember that some foods actually lower cholesterol levels. They include onions, garlic, apples and olive oil. Olive oil is also wonderful for the immune system – the body's defence against disease.

SUGGESTED DIET

As soon as you get up or in bed: Small glass of unsweetened juice or piece of fruit

Breakfast: More fruit juice and a choice of cooked breakfast: grilled bacon, fish, eggs, baked beans, cold ham, cheese, or any protein dish plus mushrooms or tomatoes. Also one slice of wholemeal bread/two crispbreads, rice cakes etc. with butter or margarine or: whole oat porridge sweetened with a few sultanas or: muesli made from whole cereals, nuts, seeds (pumpkin, sunflower etc.) or: plain yogurt with fresh fruit and nuts. You can flavour this with spices: cinnamon, ginger, crushed cardamom.

Weak tea with milk if desired or one cup weak coffee.

Two hours after breakfast: Snack: fruit, yogurt, milk, cheese and biscuits.

Lunch: Any protein dish, hot or cold;

meat, fish, cheese, eggs, chicken, sardines, tuna, pilchards etc. or any bean, lentil or nut dish

All to be eaten with lots of salad or vegetables. 1 slice of wholemeal bread or 2 crispbreads.

Two and a half to three hours after lunch: Weak tea, milk with crispbread, cheese, pâté or low sugar jam.

Half an hour before dinner: Small glass of fruit juice.

Dinner: Same as lunch, plus fruit.

Supper: Crispbreads, butter, cheese, pâté, etc. Milk drink, weak tea, herb tea.

This might look like a lot of food, but remember there is no need to eat large quantities. Small and often is the rule.

SUMMARY ·

- Don't skip meals.
- Eat regularly.
- Avoid sugary foods and drinks, and white flour; cut down on caffeine, cigarettes and alcohol.
- Always have protein in your breakfast.
- Never eat a starch-only meal (bread, cake, cereal).

If you want to learn more about blood sugar problems read: *Low Blood Sugar (Hypoglycaemia)* Martin L. Budd (Thorsons, 1986).

18 Exercise

It is often hard to convince people how important it is to exercise; they seem to think because they feel low they should be as inactive as possible. If it is confirmed that it is withdrawal causing your problems and you do not have a fever, inflamed muscles, or any condition likely to be adversely affected by exercise (check with your doctor if you are unsure), then *move*; you will delay your recovery if you don't. Take care not to rush into frenetic activity if you have been sitting around for months. Build up the amount of exercise slowly. Some people are so out of touch with their bodies that they are very resistant to the idea of exercise. You will see below why it is so important.

EXERCISE, MUSCLES AND CIRCULATION

When you slow down your circulation by inactivity, organic function – for example, the digestion – becomes sluggish; this causes constipation. Muscles are also affected, not only by lack of nourishment, but also by a buildup of crystals which are formed from the waste products of digestion. This is rather like soap powder collecting in the fibres of laundry that has not been adequately rinsed. The effect can be general muscle weakness and/or local congestion. Tension also locks these crystals into the muscles; a buildup in the shoulder area can be very painful and in turn cause you to move less. *If you do not move the muscles of the neck and shoulders, you restrict the blood supply to the head and give yourself endless problems.* You need to ask yourself, 'Am I causing my headaches, sinus problems, confusion?' The brain can become sluggish too, and when full circulation is restored symptoms of anxiety and depression can be dramatically relieved. Work at getting rid of the iron collar.

EXERCISE AND THE LYMPHATIC SYSTEM

The lymphatic system is part of the body's defence against disease. A body fluid called lymph, which relies on muscle contraction for its circulation, is carried through a complex network of small vessels carrying cellular garbage on the way. It is then passed into the bloodstream where it is processed. Unlike the circulatory system, the lymphatic system has no pump: if you don't move your muscles the lymph slows down. The results can be a collection of fluid in the tissues, particularly around the ankles if you have been sitting, and a depressed immune system. Some cells in the body which rely on lymph for their food, such as the discs separating the bones of the spine, become malnourished. Even if you have to stay in bed for some reason you can still help to circulate the lymph by gently squeezing each group of muscles in turn, and rotating the ankles and wrists. Massage can also be very helpful.

If you have been inactive for some time perhaps you could start with exercise sitting down. As you do this routine visualize anything that suggests improved circulation; slow streams becoming fast flowing sparkling rivers, pipes being unblocked, or anything that comes to mind.

EXERCISES SITTING ON A CHAIR

1. Place your feet in front of you about a foot apart. Drop your shoulders and look at the floor a few feet in front of you; this stops you shortening the muscles at the side of the neck (part of the iron collar).

2. Take one deep breath lifting your shoulders as you do so; open your mouth as you let the breath out and drop your shoulders. Imagine you are as limp as a wet sweater hanging on the washing line.

3. Breathe normally, lift the shoulders towards the ears and let them drop towards the floor – eight times if you can.

4. Keeping the arm limp, circle each shoulder in a clockwise direction eight times, and then try doing them together.

5. To stretch the neck, allow your head to fall to the right, bring it back to the centre then allow it to drop to the left – four times each side. Don't raise your shoulder to meet your ear.

6. Stretch both arms to the ceiling and let them fall loosely towards the floor.

7. Stretch out the fingers, then draw eight circles both ways with the forefingers.

8. To exercise the legs draw the same circles with each big toe in turn.

9. For the buttocks and thighs tighten these muscles and feel yourself rise in your seat.

10. Finish with shaking all over like a wet dog.

The wet dog shake is very good for people who worry about shaking in public. It takes a lot more energy to hold shaking in than to let it out. Have a good shake regularly and particularly before any social event you are worried about. If you are in trouble when you are out, find a lavatory where you can let your jaw go loose and allow yourself to shake from the head down; visualize a dog coming out of the sea and copy the movement it makes when it is trying to shake the water out of its coat.

BUILDING EXERCISE INTO YOUR DAILY LIFE

See how many gentle stretching exercises you can incorporate in your daily routine; for example, walk upstairs on your toes to stretch the backs of your legs, reach up to shelves with both hands, hold the stretch then relax. Do loose, swinging movements, running on the spot, or the wet dog shake, when you are waiting for the kettle to boil. Before getting into the bath hold the side and bend your knees a few times; rotate your ankles or massage your hands as you watch television.

Building these movements into your daily routine is useful if you do not feel up to swimming, walking or more strenuous exercise. Remember what happens to your circulation if you don't move. Perhaps the next stage could be walking briskly for thirty minutes daily and then progressing to aerobic exercise. It is easier and safer to have some supervision. Join a class or take the advice of the fitness coach at a leisure centre. The exercises might feel like a terrible chore at first but just keep going; when you feel the benefits you will be more enthusiastic. See the reference list for medical research on exercise and health.

19 *The Relaxation Response*

People who are well are in charge of their minds and bodies; they use them to full capacity and then are able to switch off and relax at will – their relaxation response is in working order.

The relaxation response in people who are tense and nervously exhausted fails because it has been overworked. Before it will function normally again it needs some help. The following scene will help you to understand why it gives up.

THE ADRENALINE EVENT

Two men are going for a run. One is in track one, the other is in track two. Imagine they are both wearing red vests. Extra energy is needed to run, so in response to their thoughts, 'I am going to run,' the brain sends a message for the muscles to contract and this squeezes the glands which produce adrenaline. Thoughts, heart-rate and breathing rate increase, blood is diverted from the internal organs to the legs to allow them to move faster, everything speeds up; the adrenaline levels are high.

The two men complete the circuit and prepare to go home.

THE MAN IN TRACK ONE

This man's muscles relax and, in response to this, chemicals which oppose adrenaline are released into the bloodstream; his heart-rate and breathing slow down, everything goes back to normal. His adrenaline levels are falling – imagine he has showered and is now wearing a blue vest. When he arrives home he is hungry and needs the bathroom. After dinner he repairs his son's bicycle, watches TV and then goes to bed and sleeps like a baby. When he wakes he feels rested.

THE MAN IN TRACK TWO

Because he has been overworking lately his relaxation response is worn out. After the run his muscles do not automatically relax, so he is deprived of the chemicals which would slow him down; his adrenaline levels have not gone down. When he arrives home, although he has showered and gone through the same motions as the other man, it is as if he is still wearing the *red* vest. He is preoccupied with worrying thoughts, he is irritable with his kids; his digestion feels upset (the extra blood is still in his legs), he does not want dinner; he tries to read the newspaper but can't concentrate. His evening is spent looking for antacid tablets, making frequent visits to the bathroom to pass urine, and chasing next door's cat from the flower borders. He has difficulty getting off to sleep, and when he does he sleeps fitfully. At 3 a.m. he wakes feeling anxious and hungry; he sleeps again and in the morning he wakes feeling anxious and stiff and sore; his muscles are still not relaxed – his adrenaline levels are still high. And it could go on like this until he has a nervous breakdown, a heart attack or some illness which will force him to slow down, *unless* he gets wise and realizes that all he has to do to don a blue vest is to slow down, to practise mechanically what his body has given up doing automatically. He must re-educate his muscles through relaxation exercises.

If the extra adrenaline can be discharged, all is well, but if it is imprisoned by tension the results can be disastrous. A person may be just sitting putting on his socks or taking the dog for a walk and be overcome by a gigantic panic attack, or feel paralysed with fear.

RETRAINING WAYWARD NERVES

The importance of correct breathing, diet and exercise have been discussed; relaxation and using the mind to heal (creative visualization) are next.

CREATIVE VISUALIZATION

If you were taught biofeedback techniques, no doubt you would be delighted with the results; lower blood pressure, slower heartbeats and all the benefits of being more relaxed. You would also think 'What a wonderful machine (or therapist)'. With practice, in your own home, you can achieve the same results by using your own wonderful machine, your mind. By giving it positive images and loving, encouraging self-talk you can change useless worrying thoughts to helpful healing thoughts.

Here is an example of how the body follows the mind:

You are sitting in the garden and you decide to do something active, say play tennis or dig a trench for the leeks. Just because you are *thinking* about being active, 'My tennis shoes are in the closet,' or, 'Harry's spade would do a better job, I'll see if he is in,' the brain is already starting to produce the chemicals you will need even before you have left your seat. You can use positive creative visualization to raise energy levels and improve performance. Conversely, negative images produce gloomy moods and tired muscles. To be able to use the mind effectively it needs to be quietened; you cannot relax if your mind is jumping hurdles.

VISUALIZATION FOR QUIETENING THE MIND

These images are only suggestions. If they don't work for you, imagine any situation where there is cheerful noise and movement that gets less and less, for example:

Imagine a tree filled with song birds. The birds fly away from the top branches, then the next branches, and so on until there is just one bird left. Concentrate on him until he flies off, then look at the branch he was sitting on, then let your mind focus on just one lovely pale green leaf.

You could also use a fairground, full of laughter and music. It is closing down for the night. The people are going home, the lights are going out.

Or think of a playground of noisy, tumbling children. It's supper time; they gradually go home. Watch the last child as he goes off with his mother; he looks sleepy.

If you have trouble stilling your mind with images, try concentrating on the feeling in your nostrils as your breath enters and leaves, or simply by repeatedly counting to ten.

TENSION RELEASE IN SECONDS

You can do this anywhere. Sit down with your back straight but not stiff, put your hands palm upwards in your lap and place your feet together flat on the floor. Droop your head a little, take one deep breath and as you let it out let your shoulders drop and allow your thighs and knees to fall outwards. Imagine a beautiful, blue sparkling light which starts about a foot above your head, let it ripple through your body and out of the soles of your feet into the floor and it will take your tension with it. If you practise this regularly you will be suprised how effective it is. You may also notice it makes your feet tingle.

THIRTY-MINUTE RELAXATION SESSION

Some people are afraid to learn to relax because they use their tension as armour – it holds their fears and hurts in (neurosis) and the frightening world out. You cannot hold on to this tension and expect to be healthy. Neurosis is discussed in detail in *Coping with Anxiety & Depression* by this author; see Further Reading.

It is a good plan to stimulate the circulation before you lie down, not only because it helps you to relax, but also because some people feel cold as tension eases. Keep a rug near you. If you become aware of your heartbeat or feel light-headed as you relax don't be alarmed, just accept it; it is quite normal. Again, if you don't like the suggested imagery, find your own. The fountain could be replaced by a waterfall, your shower, or water being poured from a jug, and the garden could, for example, be replaced by the shore, a meadow or your favourite room.

1. Do a few stretching movements and have a good shake.
2. Lie on the floor or bed, or sit supported in a chair. To stretch the neck and to ensure the chin is not jutting forward, place a small firm pillow or a few paperback books under the head.
3. Breathe slowly and gently and imagine your body is sinking into the floor.

VISUALIZATION

Imagine you are standing at a gate looking down on a lovely garden; inside the garden is wholeness, love and peace. You choose to open the gate and go inside. On the right there is a crystal-clear fountain, the sun is shining through it and you can see all the colours of the spectrum. You feel the desire to be refreshed in the fountain and imagine as you stand underneath it that a beautiful flower about a foot above your head opens and allows the water to wash through your head taking with it any drug deposits, allergens or anything harmful to your brain, eyes, ears or sinuses. Then see it cleaning your throat and down into your chest and abdomen taking anything harmful to your body with it. Watch it as it goes down your legs and see a muddy stream leave the area under the arch of the foot. The muddy water goes deep into the ground; see your feet looking soft and clean.

Now see the flower open again and this time allow the water to wash through your mind and release you from anything that has ever hurt you since before you were born; feelings of rejection, low self-worth, grief, loneliness, unhappiness about your appearance, hurtful things people have said and done, guilt about how you have hurt others, frustrations, depression, anxiety, physical pain; imagine it is all washing through you and leaving your feet again in a grey muddy stream; it completely disappears into the ground and your feet look soft and clean.

Now walk around the garden and notice if you feel lighter; you are wearing summer clothes and the grass is warm under your bare feet. You walk towards a yellow rose, and the colour surrounds your body; it fills you with tranquil feelings. Now you approach a white rose, you breathe in peace from its perfume. Your walk continues and you come to a thornless red rose bush. This rose fills you with love and forgiveness for yourself: see yourself as a little child, hug that child, stroke its hair, hold it and reassure it, tell it from now on you will do nothing to hurt it; give it another chance. See the child's face relaxed and smiling and see the small figure with loose limbs, clear skin and shining hair, skipping around the garden. As you love and forgive yourself these feelings will extend to those around you. See the garden full of the people in your life and as you offer each one a rose let it be a symbol of love and forgiveness, their forgiveness of you and your forgiveness of them.

Now continue your walk in the garden taking a gently sloping path down to the river. You pass the vegetable garden on the way and see cabbages and carrots growing; the soil looks fertile. When you reach the bottom you see a tree, there is a space in the branches where the sun is able to warm the ground. You lie down here and feel the rays of the sun travel over you. Feel a beautiful white light come over your feet; it makes them feel soft and warm. Imagine the light penetrating every cell of your body and let it travel to your calves, knees and thighs; hold the light longer over the solar plexus area or anywhere you experience pain or discomfort and then let it travel up to the chest, shoulders, neck and head. Now imagine the whole body filled with healing white light; see it radiating several feet from your body. Say to yourself several times: every day in every way I am getting better and better.

Imagine you feel your energy level rising and you stretch and slowly start to walk up the path to the rose garden. Again you pass the vegetable garden; your step is very light.

You pass the roses and the fountain and now you are at the gate and you come out of the garden. You can choose to go back there to be peaceful any time you wish.

Now wriggle your fingers and toes then raise yourself onto your side before sitting up slowly.

If you practise visualization every day you will begin to feel things changing; you will become stronger and more in charge. You may be moving away from a lifetime of negative thoughts so don't be too impatient; give it time. The idea that they are valuable human beings worthy of love is very new to many people and visualizing themselves as children often brings tears. Welcome this if it happens; it is part of the healing you need. Also don't expect to forgive everyone in the first session. One woman said: 'It took me nine weeks to give my ex-husband "a rose" but I felt so liberated when I managed it.'

You need not remember this guided imagery word for word: it is only a model for you to work from. The key factors to include are being in a peaceful place, cleansing, looking at colours, loving and forgiving yourself and others, allowing a healing light to travel over you, and repeating a positive affirmation, such as, 'every day' etc. or 'I love and approve of myself exactly as I am; I am contented and healthy'. If you like the suggested imagery and have difficulty remembering it you could put it on tape. Some people find their own voice irritating on tape; if this is your experience ask a friend, particularly someone you know who cares for you, to do it for you.

20 The Importance of Daylight, Sunlight and Fresh Air

There has been a lot of interest in the last decade in light and human health. Biologists have discovered that not only is it vital for our well-being, but also that individual requirements for light vary as much as individual needs for vitamins. As the human race has become more civilized we have spent less time outdoors, and many people travel to work by car to badly lighted buildings and then return home by car to spend an evening indoors watching TV. We do not noticeably wilt like plants in a dark corner, or like some animals which leap about at dawn and sleep at twilight, but there is no doubt that the shorter days of the autumn and winter do adversely affect some people. They experience lethargy, loss of interest in sex, and depression; as daylight increases in the spring these feelings disappear and normal energy levels return. Whilst many people can say they feel a little down in the winter, there are some people who are so seriously affected by light reduction that they have a condition known as SAD or Seasonable Affective Disorder. Sufferers become disablingly depressed, have joint pains and digestive problems, crave sweet foods and lack concentration to a degree that they cannot continue their studies or work. They have great difficulty getting out of bed in the mornings and are exhausted all day. Their lack of concentration may be so severe that they have to abandon their studies or give up work.

Fortunately it has been found that being exposed for several hours daily to light which replicates daylight cures this condition. When this light or daylight enters the eye it stimulates the pineal gland and inhibits the production of a substance called *melatonin*; normally this is only produced at night in the dark. This is what makes us sleepy.

Daylight is necessary for normal brain functioning and for the regulation of the sleep–wake cycle, so you can see that staying indoors when you are depressed or ill in any way can only compound your problems. Even if you are severely agoraphobic you could sit at an open window without sunshades; do this for a minimum of twenty minutes daily in the brightest part of the day.

SUNLIGHT

Whilst it is foolish to risk skin cancer or ageing the skin prematurely from baking in it for hours, it is equally foolish to always be covered in sun block and never allow the sun to reach the skin. Frequent exposure for short periods has many beneficial effects, including the production of Vitamin D. We also look healthier after a little sun and this increases feelings of well-being. Sunlight is also bactericidal and fungicidal.

FRESH AIR

Air that is contaminated by smoke and fumes is recognized as being harmful; there can be other causes of stale air that are not so well known.

Electrically-polluted air can be the cause not only of respiratory problems but also of headaches, irritability, digestive problems and depression. Particles in the air around us – ions – are electrically charged, positive and negative. We breathe in these particles and absorb them through the skin. If the air is overloaded with positively charged particles we can experience nasal congestion and lethargy, and feel sticky (not the same feeling as being too hot) and swollen. The oppressive feeling before an electrical storm best describes this – a restless feeling; being 'under the weather'. We can also experience this in cities where stale air is trapped between tall buildings, or in workplaces where the air is filled with positive ions from VDUs. At home this effect can be felt if we sit in badly ventilated rooms with TV sets and other electrical equipment.

Geological location and climate are other factors. Warm winds, for example the Mistral in the Mediterranean and the Santa Anna in California are loaded with positive ions and are dreaded by many people because they make them feel enervated and depressed.

After a thunderstorm the air is negatively charged; it smells fresh and we experience 'the calm after the storm', our energy returns and our mood improves. The air by the sea, waterfalls and flowing water, even by the shower, is also negatively charged and can produce a feeling of well-being.

AVOID BEING BOMBARDED WITH POSITIVE IONS

Take frequent breaks from VDU screens, fit a screen protector and buy an ionizer (a small machine that negatively charges the air). Ionizers are available in most large stores; you may have to look in a health magazine for an address for a VDU screen protector.

THE ELECTROMAGNETIC FIELD AND HEALTH

We have our own electrical system in our bodies: our hearts, muscles and nerves run on a delicate form of electromagnetic energy. Whilst we do not need to be plugged into a socket in the wall to operate, we are still electrical beings and are surrounded by an electromagnetic field. In the 1930s a Russian called Kirlian experimented with photography which clearly showed this field. One of the first people to study what he called the L-fields, or the fields of life and how they affect health, was Harold Saxon Burr, of Yale University Medical School. Dr Robert O. Becker, author of *The Body Electric* and a leading modern researcher on electromagnetic pollution, believes that man-made electromagnetic fields from power lines and electrical appliances can cause depression, a depressed immune system and other health problems. The research of this man and others suggests that disturbances in the electrical field develop before illness in the physical body. This could be the medicine of the future, the prevention and treatment of illness through correcting faults in the electromagnetic field. This knowledge is not new, and similarities can be found in ancient forms of healing. Because of the work of American nurse Dolores Kreiger, a technique which clears and energizes the electromagnetic field is taught in some nursing schools; it is known as Therapeutic Touch. She describes this in her book *Therapeutic Touch, How To Use Your Hands to Help or Heal*, (Prentice-Hall Inc., Englewood Cliffs, New Jersey 07632 USA).

ALTERNATIVE MEDICINE

Many people have turned to alternative medicine for relief of symptoms caused by withdrawal. The value of massage has already been mentioned, and homoeopathy, herbal medicine, chiropractic, reflexology, shiatsu, and aromatherapy have all been used with effect. Do seek a well-qualified practitioner and before you discontinue any medical treatment, discuss it with your physician. Alternative therapies are often used with conventional medicine as an adjunctive treatment.

21 Case Histories

Counsellors on tranquillizer phone lines are repeatedly asked, 'Have other people managed to come off this drug? Have they been on it for as long as I have?' or, 'Have other people had withdrawal symptoms when they have only taken tranquillizers for a few months?' One of the following experiences may mirror your own and answer some of your queries. It is always comforting to know someone else has been where you are and has succeeded.

Marion was prescribed diazepam when her husband died thirteen years earlier. Over the years she was so occupied raising four children that she just kept swallowing pills. She became so tired, it was an effort to get out of bed and she wondered if it had anything to do with the diazepam. Her doctor sent her to a consultant who was helpful and understanding. It was suggested that she come off her diazepam quickly in hospital. She was given other drugs to help her symptoms. She was diazepam-free two weeks later (withdrawal as rapid as this must be in hospital). She stayed in hospital for a further three weeks. Her physical appearance changed very quickly: her skin and eyes looked so much clearer. In fact she looked much younger. This often happens as people detoxify.

For a few days in hospital, as her emotions came back to life, she felt overwhelmed by grief for her husband. It surprised her that after so long there were still unshed tears.

She coped well on return home, although she was depressed for some months. After six months she looked well and apart from her sleeping pattern still not being back to normal, things were improving. The spaces between the 'down' spells were getting longer and longer, and her friends were delighted to see her sense of humour returning.

Maurice, aged 37, found it difficult to establish a normal sleeping pattern after frequent business trips to America. Nitrazepam was prescribed and he found the jet-lag easier to cope with. After three months he was not travelling so much and felt he did not need the tablets. His insomnia became worse than he had ever known it. He had palpitations, and a tight feeling in his chest, and also had digestive problems.

His doctor was kind and sympathetic but said he did not think Maurice had been on the tablets long enough for dependence to have developed. The doctor suggested going back to the full dosage to see what happened.

Maurice's symptoms were much improved when he visited the surgery a week later. His doctor said that he had discussed his problem with his partner who had said he had two patients who had experienced similar problems, although they had taken the tablets over a longer period.

Complete withdrawal took six weeks. For the following three weeks Maurice felt 'off colour' but did not have any dramatic symptoms. After that he felt well although his sleeping pattern did not return to normal for many weeks.

Ann was 27 years old when she was prescribed lorazepam (3mg). She had just learnt that her baby was mentally handicapped. She coped well with the baby but felt very down. After about four months she felt increasingly anxious. Her doctor suggested she double the dose of Ativan. The anxiety lessened, but she had frequent headaches and lost her balance very easily. She thought she was 'run down' due to increasingly heavy periods. Her husband complained she was not the same person and suggested a holiday.

Ann thought she might have more energy if she reduced her pills to half the dose. Two days later she felt very ill. She had diarrhoea, vomiting, nasal congestion, and a sore throat. The doctor diagnosed a virus. Ann had not slept for several nights so she resumed taking the full dose of lorazepam. The symptoms dramatically disappeared.

She recognized the same symptoms nine months later when she forgot to pack her pills when she stayed with an aunt. She began to wonder about the pills but her doctor assured her they were safe and non-addictive.

The heavy bleeding persisted and she was admitted to hospital for investigations. The ward sister kept her pills. Once again the strange symptoms returned: her skin burned, she felt sick, and her vision was affected. This time she was sure it was the pills but she could not convince anyone else.

A phone call to a friend, a Community Psychiatric Nurse, gave her some hope. He advised her to cut down slowly. Three months through withdrawal she noticed her periods were not so heavy and the sinus pains that had plagued her when she was on higher doses had gone. There were times during withdrawal when she felt unwell, but she began to feel her old personality coming back. Her husband remarked how different she looked. Her skin was clearer and her hair, which had become thin and dull, had grown thick and healthy again. Nine months after complete withdrawal she still had palpitations and difficulty sleeping but, apart from that, was well and delighted to be drug-free.

Andrew, aged 29, had been prescribed lorazepam for exam nerves. He had been taking them for eight years, increasing the dose twice during that time, but had not changed it during the past two years. He was then on 6mg per day.

He complained to a friend (a dentist) that he had burning spinal pain, numbness, pins and needles in his limbs, and blurred vision. The friend feared it could be multiple sclerosis, and urged him to seek medical advice. His doctor sent him to a neurologist. No cause could be found for the symptoms; all his tests were negative.

The doctor suggested a holiday. During Andrew's second miserable week, he saw a report in a local paper about a support group for people having trouble with tranquillizers. He was very relieved when the group explained what he was experiencing were withdrawal symptoms even though he was still taking the pills. His body had become accustomed to that dosage and it was crying out for more.

Three months after complete withdrawal, the spinal pain and other symptoms had disappeared. He made a weekly telephone call to the support group when he felt down or if he had suffered a panic attack. He cut down on coffee and cigarettes, and ate a balanced diet with vitamin and mineral supplements. He felt that swimming had helped him to recover, although he admits it was a tremendous effort at first to go to the local pool twice weekly. He is now very well and runs a local telephone support service for people in tranquillizer withdrawal.

Nigel, aged 49, started taking chlordiazepoxide twelve years ago when professional worries were making him anxious. Two years before he came to the group he had surgery for a hernia. It was then he decided to stop taking the pills. The surgery was uncomplicated, but his recovery was very slow. By the time he left hospital, he was suffering from severe insomnia, palpitations, anxiety worse than he had ever experienced, and a feeling of tightness in his chest. He was puzzled by how ill he felt, but thought it was weakness after the operation.

During the same year, he complained of nausea and severe abdominal pain. Hospital tests proved negative. He had his spectacles changed three times trying to correct visual disturbances. So many things were going wrong that he wondered if his wife was right when she said 'It's all in your mind,' although the severe pain he then developed in his right shoulder and his neck seemed real enough to him.

Eighteen months after withdrawal he felt better, but still had some problems. He was never tempted at any time to go back on the pills. He tried taking alcohol in the evenings, but it did not seem to help.

He feels pills did not help and made the situation even more difficult. The experience of withdrawal has changed his attitude to life. He now makes time to relax during each lunch break. What was formerly a hurried sandwich and numerous cups of coffee, is now a salad with meat or cheese and fruit. He also spends fifteen minutes lying on the office floor listening to a relaxation tape and slowing down his breathing rate. He is amazed how different he feels at the end of the day.

Grace, aged 67, had been on Tranxene (not now available on the NHS) for six years. She was first prescribed it because she was 'run down' after nursing her husband through a long illness. She had always been a strong extroverted woman who spent a lot of her time helping the young mothers and the elderly in her area. When she began to feel confused and agoraphobic she consulted her doctor. He gave her a tonic and told her to rest more. Her daughter suspected it might be the drugs affecting her and looked for information. She discovered that elderly people who are taking tranquillizers and sleeping pills should have a greatly reduced dosage because they cannot excrete them at the same rate as the young. This often leads to a buildup and oversedation. It is also important to give the correct dosage for the weight. So often, a person weighing 7 stones (98 lbs/44.5Kg) is given the same dosage as a heavyweight of 14 stones (196 lbs/88.9Kg). Grace found a telephone support line in her area and after consulting her doctor, she started to slowly cut down her dosage. The doctor said he did not know much about withdrawal but agreed to do his best. In withdrawal the agoraphobia and confusion improved, although she did have some other problems. These were headaches, slight incontinence, and a numb feeling at the base of her spine which made her feel her bottom was 'not there'. Although she was a little shaky and felt the ground was moving when she walked, she was able to go out alone after a few weeks on a reduced dosage.

Her positive attitude was a great help to her. At first she used a shopping trolley for support, then she progressed to walking with a stick and finally she walked unaided. Her humour and determination were a source of inspiration to others. She supported others in withdrawal by telephone and when heard from recently was making plans to take her grandson camping next summer.

22 What Help is There for People Coming Off Tranquillizers?

About ten years ago a London drug agency called Release noticed there were increasing numbers of people contacting them saying they were having difficulties coming off normal doses of tranquillizers and sleeping pills. The work of one of the staff, Hilary Prentice, brought public awareness to the problem and a mutual telephone support link for sufferers was organized. They no longer do this work at Release but there are now self-help tranquillizer withdrawal groups all over the country because of the work they started. There are now also support services within the statutory agencies. These are usually in drug dependence units or psychiatric departments. Neither of these are ideal for tranquillizer problems, and in the past large numbers of people have had negative experiences when they have gone for help. In the former many tranquillizer patients were treated like criminals and denied any symptomatic relief because of the 'no drugs' policy. In the latter the main complaint was that the staff were only interested in what was happening psychologically and many patients were alarmed by the lack of knowledge and concern about the physical symptoms of withdrawal. In both places in-patients complained of withdrawal being too rapid and, because of the dramatic symptoms this produced, patients often came out on more drugs than they went in with. Out-patients fared much better because withdrawal was much slower, and out-patients in pharmacology units where withdrawal programmes were tailored for individual needs, and follow-ups were protracted, did best of all. It is to be hoped that the negative experiences belong to the bad old days and that in light of more recent information, these things don't happen now.

Remember, wherever you are being withdrawn, if you feel the programme you have been given is too rapid, insist that you take it more slowly. It is *your* body – don't let anyone else tell you what it should feel like.

WHAT ARE SELF-HELP GROUPS?

These are groups of people with the same problem who meet to share information, and to encourage and support each other. The tranquillizer self-help groups in the UK and other countries grew out of need, because there was no medical help, but they can also be a source of extra support and comfort for people whose problems are acknowledged and provided for in the system.

TRANQUILLIZER SELF-HELP GROUPS

Groups can range from a few people meeting in a member's house or a church hall to large groups funded by charities, or the fund-raising efforts of members.

The magic of these groups

This is a great deal more than finding people who can explain your symptoms and tell you how to cut down your pills. The real healing is in being able to be with people who will allow you for a time to be ill, grieve over lost years on pills, and be there to reassure you with their own experience: 'I felt like that when I was at your stage in withdrawal. It *will* pass, give yourself time.' It is very moving to see how much strangers can care for each other if they are given the chance.

SHARING FEELINGS

Even if you just sit and listen in a group you will learn a lot. Where else could you be in a relaxed atmosphere and say 'I have had an awful week, I've ached all over and I've had this stupid idea that the cat was going to be run over.' Instead of getting 'What an odd woman' looks, the others will share the funny thoughts they had when they were in withdrawal, and the evening often becomes more like music hall than a group meeting. Humour is wonderful for releasing tension.

WORKING TOGETHER

This could include massaging each other's aching necks and shoulders, being together for exercise and relaxation sessions, and going swimming.

Mutual telephone support is also a very important part of self-help. There is always someone willing to talk you through a panic attack and remind you about diet, breathing etc.

WHO COMES TO TRANQUILLIZER GROUPS?

Men and women of all ages. Don't get the idea that only middle-aged women have taken these pills. There is often a high proportion of men in their thirties and forties in the groups. Men often feel more degraded than the women by the experience and often go to great lengths to hide their symptoms from friends.

ARE SELF-HELP GROUPS ALWAYS HELPFUL?

It might be necessary to discourage negative symptom swapping and be referee if there is a lot of anger about. The anger is to be expected, and usually something useful comes out of it. In fact, many have said 'I would not have chosen to go through withdrawal, but I feel I have learned so much from the experience. I am much more tolerant and appreciate life so much more.'

If you would like to start a tranquillizer self-help group an information pack is available from:

Tranquillizer Information Services,
P.O. Box 20
Liverpool
L7 6DS

To find your nearest self-help group write to:
Sarah Teevan,
Information Department,
MIND,
22 Harley Street,
London W1
(Tel: 071 637 0741)
or
Tranx (UK) Ltd (National Tranquillizer Advice Centre)
25 Masons Avenue
Wealdstone
Harrow,
HA3 5AH
(Tel: 081 427 2065)
Drop in or phone Monday to Friday 10 a.m–3 p.m.
Individual counselling and/or self-help groups for men and women in the Harrow area.
Will also refer people to groups in other parts of the UK if available.

23 *Spiritual Health*

BODY, MIND AND SPIRIT

Most people are eager to improve the health of their bodies and minds but for many, there it ends; they cannot accept that there is another vital part of them that can become malnourished; they also find it hard to accept that this could be the root of their anxiety or depression. Many become embarrassed, bored or even hostile when the spirit is mentioned; how could that possibly have anything to do with my anxiety, my death phobia, my depression?

WHAT IS THE SPIRIT?

I believe this is the part of us that continues after death; our higher self, our soul, our essence, the part of us that is precious and uniquely *us*, the part that connects with God, Allah, the Creator, the Great White Spirit, Universal Energy or whatever way you choose to think of the Divine.

It may be that depression in some people is caused by drug withdrawal and in others by a hormonal imbalance or poor diet, but there must be people whose misery comes from ignoring the frightened, sad child that is within and thereby preventing integration with the Higher Self, or Spirit. So many people are physically and emotionally sick because they are so afraid of death;

too afraid to live because of a deep, often unacknowledged fear of death, which might be years and years away for them. What a waste of life. A death phobia cannot take root in a soul that is in harmony with the personality.

SPIRITUAL HEALTH – WHERE DO I START?

When we want to improve our physical health we start with the *desire* to find the right diet, the *desire* to find suitable exercise. With the right motives the right actions follow. The same applies when we want to grow spiritually. To start, all we need is the *desire* to grow spiritually. It might be necessary to leave religion behind in order to do this. Loving others flows from loving God and loving and forgiving your inner child. Be gentle with yourself.

May Love and Light shine on you as you journey towards Self and the Divine.

Further Information

COMMITTEE ON SAFETY OF MEDICINES (UK) NUMBER 21 CURRENT PROBLEMS. JANUARY, 1988. BENZODIAZEPINES, DEPENDENCE AND WITHDRAWAL SYMPTOMS

There has been concern for many years regarding benzodiazepine dependence (*Br.Med.J.* 1980, 910–912). Such dependence is becoming increasingly worrying.

Withdrawal symptoms include anxiety, tremor, confusion, insomnia, perception disorders, fits, depression, gastro-intestinal and other somatic symptoms. These may sometimes be difficult to distinguish from the symptoms of the original illness.

It is important to note that withdrawal symptoms can occur with benzodiazepines following therapeutic doses given for short periods of time.

Withdrawal effects usually appear shortly after stopping a benzodiazepine with a short half life. Symptoms may continue for weeks or months. No epidemiological evidence is available to suggest that one benzodiazepine is more responsible for the development of dependency or withdrawal symptoms than another. The committee on Safety of Medicines recommends that the use of benzodiazepines should be limited in the following ways:

Uses

As anxiolytics

1. Benzodiazepines are indicated for the short-term relief (two to four weeks only) of anxiety that is severe, disabling or subjecting the individual to unacceptable distress, occurring alone or in association with insomnia or short-term psychosomatic organic or psychotic illness.
2. The use of benzodiazepines to treat short-term 'mild' anxiety is inappropriate and unsuitable.

As hypnotics [Sleep inducing drugs]

3. Benzodiazepines should be used to treat insomnia only when it is severe, disabling, or subjecting the individual to extreme distress.

Dose

1. The lowest dose which can control the symptoms should be used. It should not be continued beyond four weeks.
2. Long-term chronic use is not recommended.
3. Treatment should always be tapered off gradually.
4. Patients who have taken benzodiazepines for a long time may require a longer period during which doses are reduced.
5. When a benzodiazepine is used as a hypnotic, treatment should, if possible, be intermittent.

Precautions

1. Benzodiazepines should not be used alone to treat depression or anxiety associated with depression. Suicide may be precipitated in such patients.
2. They should not be used for phobic or obsessional states.
3. They should not be used for the treatment of chronic psychosis.
4. In case of loss or bereavement, psychological adjustment may be inhibited by benzodiazepines.
5. Disinhibiting effects may be manifested in various ways. Suicide may be precipitated in patients who are depressed, and aggressive behaviour towards self and others may be precipitated. Extreme caution should therefore be used in prescribing benzodiazepines in patients with personality disorders.

Useful Addresses

U.K.

Biolab Medical Unit, 9 Weymouth St., London W1N 3FF
  Information on allergy testing.

Green Farm Nutrition Centre, Burwash Common, East Sussex
TN19 7LX (Tel: 0435 882482)
  *Staffed by experienced nutritionists. Advice available via Natural
Health Hot Line, the Health Letter Service, the computer assisted
CARE Programme, and by personal nutrition consultations. Courses
and seminars on nutrition and natural health.*

Action Against Allergy, Amelia Hill, 43 The Downs, London
SW20
  *AAA (Action Against Allergy) provides an information service on all
aspects of allergy and allergy-related illness, which is free to everyone.
Supporting members get a Newsletter three times a year and a postal
lending library service. AAA can supply GPs with the names and
addresses of specialist allergy doctors. It also has a talk-line network
which puts sufferers in telephone touch with others through the NHS
and itself initiates and supports research. Please enclose s.a.e. (9"×6")
for further information.*

National Society for Research into Allergy, PO Box 45, Hinkley, Leicestershire LE10 1JY

British Holistic Medical Association, 179 Gloucester Place, London NW1 6DX

College of Health, 18, Victoria Park Square, London E2 9PF

Society for Environmental Therapy, 3 Atherton Street, Ipswich, Suffolk IP4 2LD

McCarrison Society, 24 Paddington St., London W1M 4DR

Amber Lloyd, Relaxation for Living, Dunesk, 29 Burwood Park Road, Walton-on-Thames, Surrey KT12 5LH
   Nationwide relaxation classes; also correspondence courses and training for teachers.

The Institute for the Study of Drug Dependence, 1-4 Hatton Place, Hatton Garden, London EC1N 8ND

British Acupuncture Association, 34 Alderney Street, London SW1V 4EU

National Institute of Medical Herbalists, PO Box 3, Winchester, SO22 6RB

British School of Osteopathy, Mr. Stephen Sandler, DO MRO, 1-4 Suffolk Street, London, SW1Y 4HG

Pre-Menstrual Tension Advisory Service, PO Box 268, Hove, Sussex, BN3 1RW

British Society of Medical and Dental Hypnosis, 42 Links Road, Ashtead, Surrey

Society of Teachers of the Alexander Technique, 10, London House, 266 Fulham Road, London SW10 9EL

Federation of Aromatherapists, 46 Dalkeith Road, London SE21

Wholefood, Organically Grown Produce, 24 Paddington Street, London W1M 4DR

If you write to any of the above addresses please include a SAE.

AUSTRALIA

Australian Institute of Health, Bennett House, Hospital Point, Acton, ACT GPO Box 570, ACT 2601 (062) 43 5000

Department of Community Services and Health, Suite 60 MG, Parliament House, Canberra, ACT 2600 (062) 77 7680

Alcohol and Drug Information Service (telephone: in Sydney 331 2111; outside Sydney 008 42 2599 toll free)

Women's Health Advisory Service, 187 Glenmore Road, Paddington, NSW 2021. Tel: (02) 331 1294

Australian Natural Therapeutic Association, 31 Victoria Street, Fitzroy, Melbourne

Australian Traditional Medicine Society, Rozelle, Victoria

Australian Homoeopathic Association, c/o 16a Edward Street, Gordon NSW 2027

National Herbalists Association of Australia, 27 Leith Street, Cooparoo, Queensland 4151

NEW ZEALAND

Department of Health, PO Box 5013, Wellington

Mental Health Foundation of New Zealand Inc., PO Box 37438, Parnell, Auckland

New Zealand Federation of Fitness Centres Inc., PO Box 44029, Auckland

Nutrition Society of New Zealand Inc., Dept. of Food Technology, Massey University, Palmerston North

Further Reading

Coping with Anxiety and Depression, Shirley Trickett (Sheldon Press, 1989)

Living with Fear, Isaac M. Marks, M.D. (McGraw-Hill, 1980)

Fight Your Phobia and Win, David Lewis (Sheldon Press, 1989)

No More Fears – A New Nutritional Programme to Free You from Phobias and Irrational Fears, Dr Douglas Hunt (Thorsons, 1989)

Guide to Medicines and Drugs, The British Medical Association (Dorling Kindersley, 1980)

Food Allergy and Intolerance, Dr Jonathan Brostoff and Linda Gamlin (Bloomsbury, 1989)

The Wright Diet, Celia Wright (Grafton, 1989)

Food Combining for Health, Doris Grant and Jean Joice (Thorsons, 1984)

Not All in the Mind, Dr Richard Mackarness (Pan, 1977)

Irritable Bowel Syndrome and Diverticulosis – A Self-help Plan, Shirley Trickett (Thorsons, 1990)

Cleansing the Colon, Brian Wright (available from Green Farm)

Coping Successfully with Your Irritable Bowel, Rosemary Nicol (Sheldon Press, 1989)

T. Plan Booklets by Larry Neild; Booklets on tranquillizer withdrawal, stress and nutrition: PO Box 20, Liverpool, L17 6DS

Candida Albicans: Could Yeast Be Your Problem? Leon Chaitow (Thorsons, 1985)

More Self-Help for Your Nerves and *The Latest Help for Your Nerves*, both by Dr Claire Weekes (Angus and Robertson, 1984, 1990)

The Allergy Problem, Vicky Rippere (Thorsons, 1983)

Cures That Work: A Comprehensive Guide to Alternative Medicines That Really Work, Janette Pleshette (Arrow Books, 1989)

Why Am I Afraid to Tell You Who I Am? John Powell (Fontana, 1982)

Why Am I Afraid to Love? John Powell (Argus, 1972)

Unconditional Love, John Powell (Argus, 1979)

Fully Human Fully Alive, John Powell (Argus, 1976)

Run Baby Run, Nicky Cruz (Hodder & Stoughton, 1984)

You Can Heal Your Life, Louise L. Hay (Eden Grove Editions, 1985)

Daylight Robbery – The Importance of Sunlight to Health, Dr Damien Downing (Arrow, 1988)

Electropollution, Roger Coghill (Thorsons, 1990)

Aromatherapy For Women, Maggie Tisserand (Thorsons, 1985)

Healing Your Aloneness: Finding Love and Wholeness Through Your Inner Child, Erica J. Chopich and Margaret Paul (Harper & Row, 1990)

You Can Heal Your Life, Louise Hay (Eden Grove Editions, for Mind, Body and Spirit)

References

BENZODIAZEPINES

'Aggressive Dyscontrol in Patients Treated with Benzodiazepines'
J. Clinical Psychiatry, 1988 May 49 (5): 184–8 (64 ref).

'Tranquillisers: prevalence, predictors and possible consequences'.
Data from a large United Kingdom survey, Heather Ashton
and John F. Golding British Journal Of Addiction (1989) 84,
541–546.

'Protracted Tinnitus after Discontinuation of Long-Term Thera-
peutic Use of Benzodiazepines' Usoa Busto, Pharm. D., Luis
Fornazzari M.D., FRCP(C) and Claudio A. Naranjo, M.D.
J. Clin. Psychopharmacol, Vol 8/No 5, Oct. 1988 359–362.

'Benzodiazepine Withdrawal: An Unfinished Story' Heather
Ashton DM FRCP British Medical Journal Vol 288 14 April 1984.

'Benzodiazepine Withdrawal Outcome in 50 patients' Heather
Ashton DM FRCP British Journal of Addiction (1987) 82,
665–671.

'Benzodiazepine Withdrawal: A review of the Evidence' Russell
Noyes, Jr. M.D., Michael J. Garey, M.D., Brian L. Cook, D.O., and
Paul J. Perry, Ph.D. J. Clinical Psychiatry 49:10 October 1988.

'Benzodiazepine Dependence and Withdrawal – An Update' Drug
Newsletter no 31 April 1985 Northern Regional Health Authority (UK).

'Benzodiazepines in General Practice: Time for a Decision'

J. Catalan, D.H. Gath *British Medical Journal* Vol 290 11 May 1985.

'The Psychopharmacology of Addiction – Benzodiazepine Tolerance and Dependence' Malcolm Lader DSc., Ph.D., M.D. FRC.Psych *British Association for Psychopharmacology Monograph* Oxford University Press, 1988.

'Identification and Management of Benzodiazepine Dependence' Tyrer, P. and Seivewright, N., 1984 *Postgraduate Med J.* 60 (supplement 2), 41–46.

'Benzodiazepines and Withdrawal Psychosis: Report of three cases' Sheldon H. Preskorn M.D., Lee J. Denner, M.D., JAMA, Jan. 3 1977 – Vol 237, No. 1.

ANTIDEPRESSANTS

'Problems When Withdrawing Antidepressives' *Drug and Therapeutics Bulletin* Vol 24 No. 8 21 April, 1986 (Fortnightly for doctors from the publishers of Which? Consumers Association UK).

'Addiction to Tranylcypromine' N. Griffin, R.D. Draper, M.G.T. Webb *British Medical Journal*, Vol. 283 1 August 1981.

EXERCISE

'Effects of Physical Training on Mood' Carlyle H. Folkins, School of Medicine, University of California, Davis.

√ 'Anxiety Reduction Using Physical Exertion and Positive Images' Richard Driscoll, University of Colorado, *The Psychological Record* 1976, 26 87–94.

'Mood Alteration with Swimming' Berger, B.G. and Own, D.R. *Psychom. Med.*, 45:425–433, 1983.

LIGHT

'Therapeutic Effects of Bright Light in Depressed Patients' Daniel

F. Kripke, Dept. Psychology, University of California, San Diego.
'Seasonal Variations in Affective Disorders', Rosenthal, N.E., Sack,
D.A., and Wehr, T.A. 1983. In *Circadian Rhythms in Psychiatry*.
T.A. Wehr & F.K. Goodwin, Ed.: 2:185–201. Psychopath. Box-
wood Press. Pacific Grove, Calif.
The Importance of Sunlight to Health, Dr Damien Downing (Arrow).

CANDIDA

'Invasive Candidiasis following Cimetidine Therapy' *American
Journal of Gastroenterology*, 1988 Jan 83 (1), 102–3.
'Candida Infections: An Overview' *CRC Critical Reviews in
Microbiology*, Volume 15 Issue 1.
'Urinary Tract Candidosis', *The Lancet*, October 29, 1988,
1000–1001.
'The Role of Candida Albicans In Human Illness', *Journal of
Orthomolecular Psychiatry* Volume 10, Number 4, December,
1981, 228–238.

ELECTROMAGNETISM

Electromagnetism & Life, Robert O. Becker and Andrew A. Marino,
(1982). (State University of New York Press, Albany, New York.)
'The Effects of Therapeutic Touch on Anxiety Levels of
Hospitalized Patients' Patricia Heidt Ph.D, *R.N. Nursing Research*,
Feb. 4 1980.
'Therapeutic Touch: A Facilitator of Pain Relief' Boguslawski,
Topics in Clinical Nursing Vol. 2 No 1 April, 1980, 27–39.

Index